THE NEW YORK
PUBLIC LIBRARY
AMAZING
EXPLORERS
A Book of Answers for Kids

THE NEW YORK PUBLIC LIBRARY AMAZING EXPLORERS
A Book of Answers for Kids

Brendan January

A Stonesong Press Book

John Wiley & Sons, Inc.
New York • Chichester • Weinheim • Brisbane • Singapore • Toronto

Copyright ©2001 by The New York Public Library and The Stonesong Press, Inc.

Library of Congress Cataloging-in-Publication Data

January, Brendan.
    The New York Public Library amazing explorers: a book of answers for kids / Brendan January.
       p. cm.—(The New York Public Library answer books for kids series)
    ISBN 0-471-39291-X (paper)
    1. Explorers—Miscellanea—Juvenile literature. 2. Children's questions and answers.
[1. Explorers—Miscellanea. 2. Questions and Answers.] I. Title. II. Series.

G131.J36   2001
910'.92'2—dc21   2001024240

10 9 8 7 6 5 4 3 2 1

CONTENTS

INTRODUCTION

Throughout history, explorers have ventured into the unknown, often persevering in the face of ridicule, hardship, and death. They increased scientific knowledge, exchanged ideas, established trade, and, for better and for worse, brought the world closer together.

Tens of thousands of years ago, men and women spread through Africa, Europe, and Asia in search of food, a different climate, or safety from powerful enemies. These first explorers settled the world, eventually crossing a land bridge from Siberia into the Americas and traveling by canoe to settle Australia and the islands of the South Pacific. By 11,000 years ago, humans lived on all the continents except Antarctica. Before long, empires developed and began to dominate different areas of the earth. Much exploration was fueled by the desire of these empires for wealth through trade or conquest. Explorers set off in search of both.

Other explorers braved hunger and fatigue to spread the glory of their gods. Beginning in the late eighteenth century and continuing even today, men and women have set out on exploratory expeditions and sought adventure for a variety of reasons. Some searched for knowledge, recording the earth's plant and animal life from the crushing depths of the ocean floor to the dense jungles of Africa and South America. Still others were interested simply in going places where no other human had been before. By experiencing the thundering waterfalls of Lake Victoria, or by climbing the peak of Mount Everest, they felt the joy of great achievement. Another type of explorer took an interest in people. Their endless curiosity led them to remote and often dangerous places to describe different cultures.

Explorers and adventurers often changed the course of world history by introducing one culture to another. But few of them made true discoveries. Columbus, Magellan, and other heroes of exploration did not "discover" the native peoples of the Americas and the Pacific. After all, these peoples had always known where they were. Most parts of the world have been settled for thousands of years, and many societies were informally knit together by trade. We live at a time when few places on the earth—even the frozen continent of Antarctica—remain isolated from human exploration. It may be more accurate, therefore, to call the astounding "discoveries" of the past 2,000 years "rediscoveries."

This book uses questions and answers to tell tales of explorers around the world. Unfortunately, not all the exciting stories could be included. If you want to know more about a particular explorer or exploration in general, visit the New York Public Library or your local library and check out the books listed in the bibliography and recommended reading list at the end of this book.

who were the ancient explorers? • Who were the
Phoenicians? • Who was Hanno? • What did Hanno
see? • Who was Pytheas? • Who was the greatest
general and explorer of all times? • Who
were the earliest Chinese explorers? • Who was Chang
Ch'ien? • What was the Silk Road? • Who was Fa-
hsien? • Who was Al Idrisi? • Who was Ibn
Fadlan? • Who was Al Idrisi? • Who was Brendan
the Navigator? • Who were the Vikings? • Who
was Erik the Red? • How did the Vikings spot North
America? • How did the Vikings settle North America?
• Who was Ibn Battutah? • Who was Cheng Ho?

EXPANDING THE ANCIENT WORLD

Who were the ancient explorers?

Thousands of years ago, vast empires rose and fell in Egypt, Greece, Italy, the Middle East, northern Africa, China, and India. Bold explorers from these civilizations, such as Pytheas and Hanno, ventured into unknown lands and seas. Most of them searched for new trade routes or places to settle. Today, scholars have limited knowledge of these journeys. Some accounts survive in ancient texts. Others have been pieced together by archaeologists, who have recovered and studied ancient artifacts. Though many details remain unclear, historians have managed to reconstruct some of the ancient voyages, and they prove to be just as thrilling and daring as the exploration of modern times, if not more so.

Who were the Phoenicians?

The Phoenicians were a seafaring people who dominated the Mediterranean Sea for a thousand years, from about 1400 B.C. Skilled at navigation and sailing, they established trading settlements along the coasts of Lebanon and northern Africa. The Phoenicians carried copper, tin, silver, olive oil, wine, glass, ivory, and other valuable goods from the eastern end of the Mediterranean to the western coasts of what are today Spain and France. To protect their monopoly in sea power, the Phoenicians spread rumors and false information about their discoveries and trade routes. They described oceans that boiled and monsters that lurked in the deep.

In 600 B.C., according to the Greek historian Herodotus, the Egyptian king Necho II sponsored a Phoenician expedition to sail around Africa. The ships traveled down the Red Sea and entered the Indian Ocean, where the crews planted crops, harvested them, and afterward made their way around the continent's southern tip. After three years at sea, the sailors supposedly entered the Mediterranean at its western end—completing one of the greatest feats of ancient navigation. Herodotus, however, doubted that the expedition was successful. "On their return they declared—I for my part do not believe them, but perhaps others may—that in sailing around [Africa], they had the sun upon their right hand," he wrote. Herodotus was describing the Phoenicians, who had sailed so far to the south that the sun shined from the north— a circumstance Herodotus thought was impossible.

Who was Hanno?

Hanno was an admiral from Carthage, a rich and powerful city founded by the Phoenicians on the northern coast of Africa. According to Hanno's own description of his voyages in *Periplus of Hannon*, sometime in the fifth century B.C., he led a fleet of 60 ships filled with 30,000 men, women, and children out of the city and headed west. The Carthaginians had recently battled with their rivals, the

Ancient Ships

Ships of the ancient world designed for the open sea were usually long, open craft powered by one large square sail and oars. To maneuver in and out of harbors, or if there was no wind, oarsmen rowed. The Egyptians steered their ships by manipulating a large oar secured to the right rear of the vessel—the forerunner to the rudder. In about 380 B.C., the Greek historian Xenophon described a Phoenician ship in awe. "What numbers of oars, stretchers, boathooks, marlines, and cleats for bringing the ship in and out of harbor!" he wrote. "What number of shrouds, cables, hawsers, ropes, and tackle for sailing her! And what a vast quantity of provisions!"

Greeks, in Sicily. They hoped to establish cities along the coasts of northern and western Africa and keep the Greeks away from their trading routes. At the western end of the Mediterranean Sea, the fleet passed through the Strait of Gibraltar, a channel that led to the Atlantic Ocean. Two days after leaving the Mediterranean, Hanno founded the city of Thymiaterion on what is today the coast of Morocco. After waiting for the first crops to ripen, Hanno left some ships and colonists in the harbor and sailed on. He founded five more cities. Archaeologists know the names of two, Carion Fortress and Acra. None of these cities, however, have survived.

What did Hanno see?

With two ships, Hanno continued south down the western coast of Africa and discovered the broad Senegal River where it emptied into the Atlantic. He sailed up the river into the interior of the continent and marveled at the crocodiles and hippopotamuses. Later, he wrote that the ship was attacked by "savages clad in wild beast hides. They drove us off by hurling stones at us and would not let us land." The attackers were most likely inhabitants terrified by Hanno's ship. His curiosity still unsatisfied, Hanno ordered the ship to turn south. The ship passed a landscape of boiling flame and smoke, which Hanno named Chariot of the Gods. Historians believe Hanno saw Mount Kakulima, a volcano in what is now Sierra Leone. Finally, Hanno describes sighting hairy, humanlike beasts. "Far the most of these were women with hairy bodies," he wrote, "whom our interpreters called gorillas." If Hanno did spot gorillas, it means he reached the Gulf of Guinea and may have ventured as far as Cameroon. Hanno ends his account by stating, "Provisions failing, we sailed no further." The voyage was an incredible achievement. It would take Europeans almost 2,000 years to repeat Hanno's feat.

Who was Pytheas?

Pytheas was an astronomer, navigator, and geographer raised in the third century B.C. in the Greek colony of Massalia (present-day Marseilles), a city on the southeastern coast of France. At that time, the trade rivalry between the

Phoenicians and the Greeks was intense. Phoenician warships closely guarded what is now called the Strait of Gibraltar to prevent Greek traders from reaching the ports of northwestern Europe. Instead of an easy sea voyage, traders had to transport goods overland through France. Pytheas hoped to break the Phoenician monopoly. Eventually, Pytheas avoided the Phoenicians and passed safely through the strait. He was probably attempting to find a sea route to transport tin, which was mined in the British Islands and was vital to the production of bronze. After sailing around the Iberian peninsula, which includes Spain and Portugal, Pytheas followed the coast of France north. Later, a Greek historian named Polybius would preserve Pytheas's account of his journey.

Pytheas stopped in what is now Cornwall, the southwestern section of England, and described the mines where tin was extracted from the earth. He wrote that the inhabitants, called Celts, were friendly, and he enjoyed their beer and honey wine. He also noted that England had miserable weather, a complaint that has echoed down to our times. After spending an unknown amount of time in England, Pytheas sailed north between Ireland and Scotland and entered the North Sea. At this point, Pytheas landed on either Iceland or Norway. (Scholars are not certain.) Pytheas called the land Thule, and he described the 24-hour polar days as the "ever-shining fire." Incredibly, Pytheas sailed even farther north, only stopping when he encountered a place where land, air, and sea appeared to be combined

Ancient Views of the World

Ancient civilizations, such as those in Egypt and Mesopotamia (modern-day Iraq), believed that the earth was a flat disk surrounded by ocean and covered by the dome of the sky. In the sixth century B.C., the Greek philosopher and mathematician Pythagoras suggested that the earth was in fact a sphere, a theory accepted by the famous philosopher Aristotle. In the second century A.D., Ptolemy in Alexandria made a map of the world. He included Europe, the Middle East, and the coast of India, but vastly underestimated the size of the world's oceans. His view of the world would dominate western science for another 1,500 years.

together in a "jelly-fish" kind of ice. Some scholars believe that Pytheas ran into an area of ice sludge and fog in the Arctic Ocean. After this, Pytheas finally returned south and wrote of his journeys in a volume titled *On the Ocean*, which has been lost. In it Pytheas demonstrated his keen observation powers. He calculated the distance from north Britain to Marseilles at 1,050 miles, just short of the actual figure of 1,120 miles. He also theorized that the moon was responsible for the tides and noted that the North Star is not always above the North Pole. No other ancient explorer is known to have followed his route, and at the time his accounts were dismissed as exaggerated stories.

Who was the greatest general and explorer of the ancient world?

Alexander the Great, born in Macedon north of Greece in 356 B.C., is remembered as the greatest general of the ancient age. He was also its greatest explorer. Bold, fearless, and full of curiosity, Alexander led his Greek army to victories in a steady march across the Middle East. He conquered Egypt, penetrated the Sahara desert, and sent a party up the Nile River to discover why it flooded every year. In his relentless campaign to crush his enemies, the Persians, Alexander swept through Turkey and into Mesopotamia. Along the way, he instructed scribes to describe the lands, their cities, and their people. After capturing Babylon, Alexander and his army marched into the wild, mountainous region of Afghanistan, where he founded several cities, all named after himself. Though he had already passed the limits of the known world, Alexander could not resist crossing the Hindu Kush, a formidable mountain range 500 miles long with peaks more than 25,000 feet tall. In India, Alexander smashed a local Indian army and marveled at its elephants.

But even as Alexander continued lusting after new discoveries in the East, his men began to rebel. Alexander dreamed of continuing on to China; his men dreamed of going home to Greece. Finally, Alexander gave in, though a report said he retreated to his tent and broke down in sobs of fury and disappointment. Instead of returning as he had come, he marched south to the coast of the Indian

In 332 B.C., Alexander founded a city on the western edge of the Nile delta in Egypt. The city, called Alexandria, became capital of Egypt and a center of trade and Greek culture. It also was the site of a great lighthouse, one of the Seven Wonders of the Ancient World. Little of the ancient city has survived.

continued on page 10

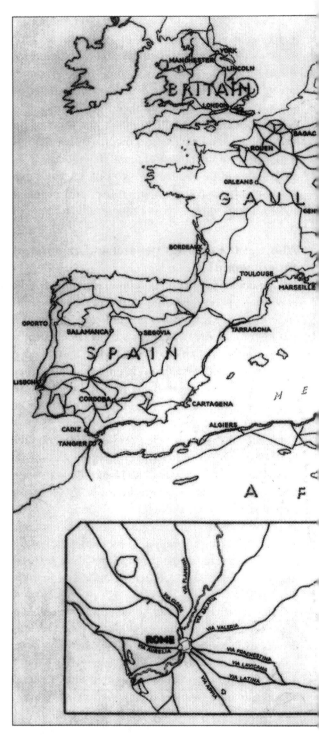

In the third century B.C., the explorations of Pytheas had been spurred by his desire to find a new route to the rich tin mines of Cornwall, England. But by the the second century A.D., at the height of the Roman Empire, a network of well-maintained roads stretched from one end of the Mediterranean to the other. Ancient explorers began to turn their attention to China and the East instead of Europe.

HIGHWAYS
OF THE
ROMAN EMPIRE

continued from page 7

Ocean, where he divided his army into three parts. One was to return by ship, while the other two would march overland. The middle route, which Alexander personally led, was across the barren, lifeless stretch of land called the Makran Desert—an area avoided by travelers to this day. Alexander's men were decimated by the burning sun and parched landscape, but Alexander survived. When he returned to Babylon, Alexander had been in the East for seven years and had conquered most of the known world. But instead of resting, Alexander ordered a fleet to prepare to sail around the Persian coast. Alexander's dream was never realized. At age 33, he died of disease.

Who were the early Chinese explorers?

While the empires of the western world were expanding eastward, explorers from the Chinese Empire were venturing west. The first motive of the Chinese was to establish contacts in the Middle East and India for alliances and trade.

This image of a coin shows a profile of Alexander the Great, whose relentless quest for adventure and empire made him one of the greatest explorers of the ancient world. In a brief ten years, Alexander conquered most of the known world before he fell ill and died at the age of 33.

But a second motive emerged after A.D. 400—religion. Buddhism emerged in India in the sixth century B.C. and spread to China. Later, Chinese pilgrims would travel to India to discover more about the Buddha and his teachings.

Who was Chang Ch'ien?

Chang Ch'ien was one of the earliest and most famous Chinese explorers. In 138 B.C., the Emperor Wu Ti sent Ch'ien west on a mission to find allies. But he was captured by China's enemy, the Huns, and spent ten years in captivity. He escaped and made contact with the Yüeh-chih, a nomadic tribe in what is today Afghanistan. Ch'ien reported back to the Chinese emperor in 116 B.C. Wu Ti sent him on another mission the following year, this time to the Wu-Sun, a tribe that lived in what is today southern Russia. On this journey, Ch'ien compiled information on Fergana, a city in Uzbekistan, and India and Parthia—modern-day Iran. When Ch'ien's journeys were complete, China had made contact with the civilization established by Alexander the Great. The Roman and Chinese empires began to exchange goods.

What was the Silk Road?

The Silk Road was a 4,000-mile-long trading route between the civilizations of Rome and China. Caravans carrying Chinese goods—especially silk—traveled out of northwest China, around the burning desert sands of Takla Makan, over the Pamir Mountains north of India, into Mesopotamia, and finally arrived at the eastern end of the Mediterranean. No one group made the trip. Instead, the goods were passed from one group to another, often taking years to reach their destination. The groups inhabiting the middle of the Silk Road made enormous profits from the trade, and they tried to prevent any direct contact between China and the Roman Empire.

Who was Fa-hsien?

Fa-hsien was born in the Chinese city of Shansi sometime in the fourth century A.D. As a young man, Fa-hsien became an avid follower of Buddha. He resolved to visit India to see where the Buddha had lived his life and visit temples and shrines of Buddhist teaching. According to an

In A.D. 97, the Chinese sent a special ambassador named Kan Ying to open relations with Rome. He made it as far as Parthia—modern-day Iran—where the Parthians told him it would take two more years to reach Rome. Discouraged, Kan Ying went no farther.

account written by Fa-hsien titled *Fo Kua Chi* (Record of Buddhist Kingdoms), it took him more than five years to journey from China to central India. "In the desert were numerous evil spirits and scorching winds, causing death to anyone who would meet them," he wrote. "Above there were no birds, while on the ground there were no animals. One looked as far as one could in all directions for a path to cross, but there was none to choose. Only the dried bones of the dead served as indications." Fa-hsien wrote of mountains where he climbed sheer cliffs 8,000 feet tall. The height, he wrote, made him "dizzy." Fa-hsien made invaluable recordings of Buddhist life as he traveled down the Ganges River Valley in India and finally returned to China via ship.

Who was Hsüan-tsang?

Hsüan-tsang, a Chinese Buddhist monk, was born in A.D. 602. While studying Buddhist religious texts, Tsang noticed contradictions. Troubled, he decided to visit India, the source of Buddhism, and resolve the discrepancies. In 629, Tsang began his trek by crossing north of the Takla Makan, a vast wasteland of barren sand. His companions and guide soon abandoned him. Pressing on alone with his horse, Tsang followed animal trails and camel bones. He lost his way but his horse, perhaps detecting water, led him to Turfan, a desert oasis. Next, Tsang crossed over the Hindu Kush mountain range into Pakistan and reached the sacred valley of the Ganges River in India, the holy land of Buddhism. In India, Tsang visited the major sites associated with the Buddha. He wrote of giant libraries filled with

The Rise of Islam

In the seventh century, an Arabian named Muhammad founded the religion of Islam. With astonishing speed, the religion spread from the Arabian peninsula to India, Turkey, Egypt, North Africa, and Spain. With the Islamic Empire straddling much of the known world, Muslim traders and travelers observed life from Africa to China. Travel was also encouraged because Muslims are supposed to make at least one pilgrimage to the holy shrine of Mecca (in present-day Saudi Arabia) during their lifetime.

books and merchants who traded silks and carpets with Persians in the Middle East. Tsang spent 16 years in India. When he returned to China, he was received by the Chinese emperor, who was so impressed with Tsang's accounts that he offered him a post in his court. Tsang respectfully declined and devoted the rest of his life to translating into Chinese the massive amount of Buddhist documents that he had carried from India.

Who was Ibn Fadlan?

Many Arab travel narratives from the 800s and 900s are filled with fantastic stories of doubtful accuracy. One traveler named Ibn Fadlan, however, gave a very level account of his visit to the Bulgars, a people in southern Russia who had recently converted to Islam. In A.D. 921, Fadlan was sent to advise the Bulgars on their new religion. While he stayed with the Bulgars, Fadlan observed the Rus, a people who had descended from Vikings. Fadlan described the Rus as a dirty, primitive group that still worshipped pagan gods. With grim detail, Fadlan described a king's funeral, where a female slave was gruesomely sacrificed and laid alongside the dead chief in a ship. The ship was then burned.

Who was Al Idrisi?

Al Idrisi was a Muslim geographer and mapmaker who lived in the Christian kingdom of Sicily in about A.D. 1100. Idrisi had studied in Spain and had traveled extensively in North Africa, Europe, and the Middle East. Supported by the Christian king Roger II of Sicily, Idrisi drew on Greek and Arab sources to create a map of the heavens and the world. He sent out expeditions to confirm his calculations and he relied on Arab sea captains, who told him that Africa was in fact surrounded by water. He engraved a map of the world on a 12-by-5-foot silver plate and created another globe of the heavens. He also wrote a book about his travels, commonly called *The Book of Roger* in honor of his king. The Arabic title translates as "The Pleasure Excursion of One Who Is Eager to Traverse the Regions of the World." Idrisi's work represented the summit of Arabic mapmaking.

Arab Sea Vessels

Arab merchants sailed the oceans in swift ships with lateen-rigged sails—meaning the sails were hung diagonally, rather than straight, as in western ships. These fast-moving vessels allowed the Arabs to dominate trading routes between China, the Middle East, and Europe.

Who was Brendan the Navigator?

Sometime between A.D. 500 and 800, Christian monks from Ireland voyaged to Europe and possibly across the Atlantic Ocean to spread Christianity. They sailed in curraghs, open wicker-frame boats covered with animal hides. In the 500s, a monk named Brendan sailed to the Hebrides Islands off the coast of Scotland, to the Scottish mainland, and possibly to Wales and Brittany, France. According to an Irish epic called *Navigatio Brendani* (Voyage of Brendan), he also led an expedition into the Atlantic Ocean to the "Promised Land of the Saints." Historians have speculated that the land is Iceland or the Canary Islands off the northwest coast of Africa. He is remembered today as St. Brendan the Navigator.

This medieval depiction of St. Brendan shows him voyaging into the Atlantic Ocean.

Who were the Vikings?

The Vikings were fierce, hardy, and brave people who lived in Scandinavia, the frigid northern lands of Europe. Traveling in longboats, long, narrow ships with square sails and oars, the Vikings plundered Scotland, Wales, England, Ireland, and the coasts of northern Europe from about A.D. 800 to about A.D. 1100. They sacked monasteries, slaughtered the monks, looted the gold, and hauled food back to their ships before disappearing again onto the dark waters of the North Sea. From about A.D. 790, the Vikings terrorized northern Europe, even traveling east and south through Russia to make contact with Arab traders in Baghdad. In the 800s and 900s, land in Scandinavia became scarce, and some Vikings began to settle in foreign lands. Driven by the need for land and a hunger for wealth and adventure, these intrepid people turned westward and became the first Europeans to discover and colonize North America, almost 500 years before Columbus sailed.

Who was Erik the Red?

About A.D. 860, Viking sailors reported that a large but uninhabited island lay due west of Norway. An expedition soon confirmed that an island of icy fjords, mountains, and grassy plains lay open to settlement. By A.D 930, 20,000

Tim Severin

Tim Severin was born in 1940 and studied at Oxford University, England. Intrigued by early exploration, he attempted journeys in ships that followed the same design and were constructed from the same materials as ancient ships. In 1976–1977, Severin demonstrated that St. Brendan could have crossed the Atlantic Ocean in a curragh by building one and sailing it from Europe to North America himself. Departing from Ireland, he sailed to Iceland, on to Greenland, and finally reached Newfoundland. He then returned to Ireland by the same route. Severin also confirmed that the account later written about St. Brendan's voyage was consistent with his own experience. To prove that the Chinese may have journeyed to North America thousands of years ago, Severin built a bamboo craft and tried to sail it across the Pacific Ocean in 1995. That voyage, however, was unsuccessful, and Severin was forced to turn back.

Viking settlers had crowded onto the island, called Iceland. One of them was an exile from Norway called Erik the Red. Erik was passionate, and his explosive temper matched the intensity of the fiery color of his hair and beard. He killed a man during an argument and was expelled from the town. He moved, settled, and then killed two of his neighbor's sons in another quarrel. The Vikings ordered Erik to leave Iceland for three years. Erik faced a difficult decision. He couldn't return to Norway, but he was unable to remain in Iceland. Boldly, Erik decided to sail west with his family and 30 settlers. He had heard stories of yet another island in the Atlantic. After four days at sea, Erik sighted a coast of mountains locked in ice and snow. Erik ordered the ship to sail south, hoping to find arable land. He soon rounded the island's southern tip and spotted fields covered with grass. Erik ordered the ships to stop there, and the families began building homes and planting crops. After three years, Erik returned to Iceland to find more settlers. He shrewdly called the new land "Greenland," realizing that the attractive name would entice colonists. In A.D. 986, 14 ships with 450 Vikings returned with Erik and settled on farms that soon stretched along 120 miles of Greenland coastline.

How did the Vikings spot North America?

While sailing from Iceland to Greenland, a Viking boat was blown off course to the west and reported the existence of a shadowy, unknown land. News of the sighting soon reached the Vikings in Greenland. Leif Eriksson, the son of Erik the Red, was just as brave and curious as his father. He gathered 35 Vikings for a sea journey to learn more about this mysterious place.

How did the Vikings settle North America?

After days at sea, Leif spotted a barren island, which he called Helluland, or "Flatstone Land." Flatstone Land is called Baffin Island today and sits off the coast of northern Canada. Leif and the Vikings continued south, sighting a wooded land with flat beaches. Leif called it Markland, or "Wooded Land." The Vikings sailed on and found a suitable place on an island to pass the winter. They erected a small village, which Leif named after himself—Leifsbudir. They

Leif Eriksson, a Norseman, led the first Viking expedition to North America and established a settlement on Newfoundland.

were delighted to find streams choked with salmon and vines heavy with berries growing nearby. When the Vikings left the next spring, Leif called the land "Vinland," meaning Wineland. Today, it is called Newfoundland. The next spring, Leif's brother, Thorvald, followed Leif's route. The voyage was less fortunate. The Vikings fought a battle with American Indians, and Thorvald died from arrow wounds. In 1009, about 250 Vikings settled in Vinland, the

With a favorable wind, the Vikings could sail from Greenland to their settlement in North America in two weeks. In 1998, a group of men built a replica Viking ship and attempted the voyage. It took them three months.

first European settlement in North America. But hostile Indians doomed the colony and it was abandoned just four years later. The Viking population on Greenland also eventually dissipated in the late 1400s, when winters became colder and a combination of disease and Eskimo attacks killed off the population.

News of the Viking discovery of North America did not spread to the rest of Europe. When other Europeans again sailed into the Atlantic Ocean in the 1400s and 1500s, they were surprised by what they found.

Who was Ibn Battutah?

Ibn Battutah was born in Morocco, on the northwest coast of Africa, in 1304, and became one of the greatest travelers in history. As part of his religious duty as a Muslim, he set off on a pilgrimage to Mecca in Saudi Arabia in 1325. On this journey, Battutah felt the first thrill of what would become a lifelong love for travel. Vowing to "never take the same road twice," Battutah trekked more than 75,000 miles over the vast Islamic Empire, which stretched from Spain to India. He wrote down his experiences in the *Rihlah*, one of the most famous travel books ever written.

Battutah stayed in Mecca for three years, studied law, and set out for Baghdad in Mesopotamia. Leaving Baghdad he traveled south to Yemen and sailed down the east coast of Africa. He established trading contacts and grew wealthy. He turned north and journeyed into Turkey, where local rulers welcomed him as a Muslim scholar. Battutah then moved east, crossing through Iran, Georgia, Armenia, and Afghanistan. Harsh weather and the biting cold did not deter him. At one time, he had to wear three coats and two pairs of trousers. The bulky clothing made him so unwieldy that he had to be assisted onto his horse. He traveled through the Hindu Kush mountains and entered India. The ruler of Delhi made him ambassador to China. Battutah loaded a ship with gifts for the Chinese Emperor, but he was shipwrecked, and his gifts and his possessions were scattered into the ocean. He eventually reached Peking, but the emperor was no longer there. Unbowed, Battutah explored Ceylon, Bengal, and Java before finally returning to his home in Morocco, where he was received as a hero. He spent the last years of his life relating his extraordinary travels to a scribe. He died peacefully at the age of 73.

Who was Cheng Ho?

While the Islamic Empire spread from Spain to India, Chinese ships were traveling to Japan, Arabia, and even to the southern tip of Africa. The Chinese sailors traveled in junks—some of which were giant ships that displaced more than 1,000 tons. (Columbus's ships averaged about 100 tons in size.) Scholars are not certain exactly when the Chinese reached the coast of Africa, but some texts suggest as early as the 800s. In the 1400s, a Chinese explorer named Cheng Ho led seven sea expeditions, reaching the islands of Java and Sumatra, the coasts of India, and ports in Persia, where the Muslims were astonished by the size of the Chinese fleet. Squadrons of Cheng Ho's ships may have traveled around Africa and explored its western side, decades before the Europeans would reach the continent's southern tip. But these expeditions were to be China's last. Confucianism, which scorned the outside world, was becoming the dominant philosophy in China, causing the Chinese to abandon their explorations and turn inward. At about this time, Europe was fully emerging from its former isolation.

Who was Marco Polo?

Marco Polo was born in Venice, Italy, in 1254 to a family of jewel merchants. When Marco was 17, his father and uncle took him on a journey that would last 24 years and cover much of the western and eastern worlds. His later accounts of his travels in the Middle East and China would spread through Europe, inspiring the imaginations of kings and explorers and helping to launch the Age of Exploration centuries later.

Marco, his father, and his uncle left Venice in 1271. For the next three years, they traveled the spice route through Turkey, Iran, Afghanistan, the Pamir Mountains, and the searing sands of the Gobi desert. Marco wrote down notes of his observations—black oil burned for light, blinding sandstorms that seemed to sing, and horse-riding bandits who attacked and captured much of their caravan. The

Polos barely escaped with their lives. After traveling 8,000 miles, the Polos arrived in Cathay, or China, ruled by the powerful Kublai Khan.

What did Marco observe in the East?

Marco was stunned by the magnificence of the khan's royal court. The king entertained 40,000 guests at banquets that served dozens of courses of meat and fish. The khan grew fond of the intelligent young Italian, and he ordered Polo to various parts of his empire as his agent. Marco saw the wonders of the eastern world—gorgeous palaces, exquisite silks, porcelain vases, and paper money, which was unheard of in Europe, and hunted game in a vast park with cheetahs and falcons. The khan ruled his 34 provinces by sending messages through an elaborate network. About every 25 miles, couriers and fast horses awaited the khan's messages. When one arrived, they carried it quickly to the next post, ensuring that the ruler's orders arrived quickly and safely. Marco also observed the lifestyle of the Tartars—nomadic horsemen who lived on the vast, flat Asian steppes. They carried tents that collapsed easily for transportation and were covered in felt waterproofed with animal fat. They also dehydrated milk into powder. On a long journey, the Tartars mixed the powder with water in a pouch. After a day of travel, the mixture had become a thin gruel that they ate for dinner.

Kublai Khan valued Marco so greatly that at first he refused to allow the Polos to return to Europe. In 1292, however, the khan reluctantly gave them permission to leave. This time, the Polos returned mostly by sea, sailing around the coast of India.

How did Marco inspire other explorers?

When Marco Polo returned to Venice in 1295, he told fantastic tales of what he had seen, drawing scorn and accusations of exaggeration. Marco's descriptions appeared to the Venetians to be the wild ramblings of a child's imagination. Marco, however, insisted that his stories were true. On his deathbed, Marco said, "I have not told half of what I saw." Today we might not know the name Marco Polo had he not been captured while battling Venice's rival city,

Genoa. In prison, Marco shared his stories with a fellow prisoner named Rustichello of Pisa. Rustichello, a writer of romances, wrote down Marco's stories and printed them in a book, *The Description of the World*. Later, these stories would inspire a whole generation of European explorers to look for the wealth and wonders of the East. One sea captain read through the book and took careful notes. He even kept the book with him when he embarked on a daring voyage west across the Atlantic Ocean. His name was Christopher Columbus.

What was the European Age of Exploration? ◆ What
aused the Age of Exploration? ◆ What were the
ndies? ◆ Who was Christopher Columbus? ◆ What
did Columbus find? ◆ Who was the first European
explorer to reach America? What was
he Treaty of Tordesillas? Who was John Cabot? ◆
How did Cabot son Sebastian continue exploration?
◆ Who was Ferdinand Magellan? Magellan
ircumnavigate the world? ◆ Who was Giovanni da
Verrazano? ◆ Who were the conquistadors? ◆ Who
was Vasco Núñez de Balboa? ◆ Who searched for the
ountain of Youth? ◆ How did Cortés encounter the

DISCOVERING NEW LANDS

What was the European Age of Exploration?

We know of many explorers and travelers from the
Middle East, Africa, and China before the 1400s. But during
the fifteenth century, advances in exploration occurred in a
relative backwater of the world—western Europe. At the
dawn of the 1400s, most Europeans tilled the soil and had
little knowledge of the world beyond their villages. The
coasts of Africa were uncharted. The continents of North
and South America were unknown to Europeans. China,
Japan, and India were mysterious lands described in legend and song. Except for generations of secretive fishermen, sailors dared not venture into the dark and unmapped
seas, where many people believed that monsters lurked
and the sea boiled.

But over a period of 100 years, from about 1450 to 1550,
a handful of European explorers would encounter and chart
much of the world—the coasts of Africa and Asia, North
America, South America, and the vast Pacific Ocean, dotted
with islands. The medieval map was replaced with the globe
inscribed with the rough outlines of the continents.

What caused the Age of Exploration?

Several technological developments and changes in attitude spurred the Age of Exploration—better ships, improved

navigation, a new ambition to learn more about the world. But most important, Europeans wanted exotic spices to enliven their meals and preserve their meats, which spoiled quickly without refrigeration. Since Roman times, cinnamon, ginger, nutmeg, and pepper had been brought to Europe from the lands of the East, where most spices flourished in the warm and moist climate. The trade route over land was long, arduous, and dangerous. Spices were carried by Arab traders through the mountains and deserts of the Middle East and transported by ship over the Mediterranean Sea to Italian ports, especially Venice. Each time the spices were handed to another carrier, they increased in price. By the time they arrived in European cities, the spices were extremely expensive. Pepper was measured in silver and nutmeg was as valuable as gold. To win the wealth of the trade routes for themselves, Europeans began searching for a water route to the "Indies."

What were the Indies?

Japan, China, India, and the hundreds of islands scattered among them were lumped together under the name "Indies" by Europeans.

Who was Christopher Columbus?

Little is known about Columbus's early years, except that he was born in 1451 and raised in the Italian city of Genoa. Genoa was a busy port, where the docks bristled with ship masts and the streets were crowded with sailors and sea captains. Columbus went to sea with the small fleets that carried goods from Genoa to the rest of Europe. In 1476, his ship was attacked by French and Portuguese men-of-war. After his ship sunk, Columbus swam six miles to the coast of Portugal. The disaster turned out to be the luckiest event in Columbus's life. He traveled to Lisbon, a Portuguese port city that was the center of ocean exploration and trade. There Columbus learned mathematics, navigation, and astronomy, and joined several sailing expeditions. In the 1480s, Columbus pondered a radical idea. Knowing that Earth was a sphere, he reasoned that the Indies could be reached by sailing west across the Atlantic Ocean. Until then, European sailors pointed their ships south and east, trying to reach the Indies by sailing around or through Africa. For years, Columbus tried to convince European monarchs to finance his voyage. The kings turned the matter over to their advisers. Some thought it too risky. Others correctly plotted that Japan and China were thousands of miles away and too far for a sea journey. In England, King Henry VII's advisers bluntly dismissed Columbus's plans as "a joke." Columbus finally found a sympathetic audience in Queen Isabella of Spain, but at the time the Spanish were busy fighting the Moors (Spanish Muslims) in southern Spain. In January 1492, the last Moors surrendered, and Isabella and her husband, King Ferdinand, could provide Columbus with supplies, sailors, and three ships for his voyage—the *Niña*, *Pinta*, and *Santa Maria*.

What did Columbus find?

For weeks, the three tiny ships sailed west. As the sea stretched on, the crews began to grumble and whisper of mutiny. Columbus alternately encouraged, exhorted, and threatened them. On October 12, 1492, after six weeks at sea, a lookout on the *Pinta* spotted a sliver of beach glowing in the moonlight. Land! Columbus named the island San Salvador—"Holy Savior." After dawn, Columbus and his companions marched onto the beach and planted a staff of banners into the sand, claiming the land for Spain. Convinced he had indeed found the Indies, Columbus named the people of the islands "Indians," a name the native people of North and South America have carried for centuries afterward. Columbus spent the next two months exploring the Bahama Islands and the coasts of Cuba and Hispaniola. He captured six Indians and stowed on his ships a collection of gold trinkets, colorful parrots, and other evidence of his discoveries. Then he set sail for Spain. When he arrived in March, he was greeted as a hero and news of the discovery spread through Europe.

Who was the first European explorer to find a sea route to the Indies?

While all of Europe discussed Columbus's discoveries with excitement, the Spanish began to regard Columbus as a failure. They were unimpressed by Columbus's descrip-

Despite four voyages, Columbus never realized that he had landed on a whole new continent. He died believing that he had found a route to the Indies.

The Art of Navigation

For centuries, European sailors navigated between the ports of the Mediterranean Sea. Because of Italy's prominence in trade, many of the first great explorers—Columbus, John and Sebastian Cabot, Vespucci, and Verrazano—were Italians. The ancient sea captains directed their ships using the stars, the sun, their experience, and various instruments, including the astrolabe, which allowed navigators to measure the angle of the sun and stars and determine their latitude. But in the eleventh century, a new device, the compass, allowed sea captains to navigate accurately regardless of weather or time of day. Nevertheless, experienced navigators also continued to rely on a tactic called "dead reckoning." By estimating the speed of the ship, the navigator calculated the distance passed in a day and recorded it on a map. Dead reckoning was never exact and relied largely on the instinct of the sailor and his knowledge of the sea.

tions of the gorgeous, unspoiled land. They wanted gold and spices, and even after four voyages, Columbus could only report of lush jungles and villages of mud huts.

While Spain concentrated on sailing west, a group of Portuguese explorers ventured south, feeling their way along the coast of Africa. Estevão da Gama was given command of an expedition but died before the voyage began. The commission passed to his son, Vasco da Gama, a captain who successfully had fought the French off the coast of Guinea. In 1497, da Gama led four ships around the stormy southern tip of the continent and into the Indian Ocean. In May 1498, da Gama landed in Calicut, the richest and most powerful port near the southern tip of India. Da Gama had discovered a sea route to the Indies. To his delight, the warehouses of Calicut were filled with gold, silver, rubies, pearls, sapphires, fine silks, and sacks of spices. The king of Calicut received da Gama with great ceremony and wrote a message on a palm leaf for his journey back to Europe. "My country is rich in cinnamon, cloves, ginger, pepper, and precious stones," he wrote. "That which I ask of you in exchange is gold, silver, corals, and scarlet cloth."

Da Gama returned to Portugal with his ships crammed full of goods. His stores of pepper alone fetched 27 times the price he had paid in India. The Venetians and Arab traders were stunned, but their monopoly on spices was decisively broken. Da Gama, like Columbus in Spain, was hailed as a national hero. His navigation instruments, maps, and logs of the voyage were locked up and kept under close guard. Portugal had no intention of sharing the riches of eastern trade with its European rivals. The other European powers would have to find the sea route to India for themselves.

What was the Treaty of Tordesillas?

Spain and Portugal were soon disputing each other's claims in the New World. In 1493, Pope Alexander VI approved a borderline stretching from the North Pole to the South Pole. It ran about 300 miles west of the Cape Verde Islands. All claims to the west of the line were ceded to Spain. Everything to the east was Portugal's. The two countries signed the treaty on June 7, 1494. In 1506, the Portuguese declared that the treaty was unfair, and the line was moved about 1,000 miles west of Cape Verde, allowing the Portuguese to found a colony in Brazil, South America. None of the other seafaring countries—England, France, Sweden, or Holland—recognized the treaty.

Who was John Cabot?

Little is known about the early years of John Cabot. By 1461, Cabot had become a Venetian citizen and worked for a trading firm. He gained knowledge of the sea by traveling between Venice and the eastern Mediterranean region, even venturing as far as Mecca, the great Muslim center in Arabia. Some historians believe that Cabot was thinking about reaching the Indies by sailing west when Columbus returned from his first voyage in 1493. Cabot reasoned that sailing farther north would be a shorter trip due to the curvature of the earth. In March 1496, the English king Henry VII, eager to catch up to Portugal and Spain in exploration, authorized Cabot to pursue his plan. In May 1497, Cabot left Bristol in a tiny ship with his son, Sebastian, and 20 sailors. About a month later, Cabot sighted land, possibly the northern tip of Newfoundland, the giant island off the coast of Canada. He went ashore with his men—the first English on North American soil—and claimed the land for King Henry VII. Convinced that he had discovered the Indies, Cabot returned to England in triumph. He reported that the land was covered with timber and the seas filled with fish. He called the territory "Newfounde Lande." Excited by his success, Cabot planned another voyage, this time with five ships and more than 200 men. He was determined to reach Japan. Little is known about this second voyage except that it left sometime in 1498 and that one ship stopped in Ireland for repairs. The other four ships, with Cabot aboard one of them, never returned.

How did Cabot's son, Sebastian, continue exploration?

Sebastian did not accompany his father on the disastrous voyage in 1498. But in 1508, Sebastian led an English expedition to North America. Following the route of his father, Sebastian reached Newfoundland and sailed north,

How Did America Get Its Name?

Amerigo Vespucci, an Italian, moved to Spain in 1492 and opened a business to finance ship voyages. Vespucci was most likely in Spain when Columbus returned from his first triumphant voyage. As more voyages were planned, Vespucci assembled gear, ships, crews, and funds. Eventually, Vespucci wearied of hearing others describe the wonders of the "New World." He resolved to see these lands for himself. When and how often Vespucci sailed is still debated by historians. He made at least two voyages between 1499 and 1504. The first, for Spain, sailed along the northern part of South America and into the Caribbean. The second expedition, this time in the service of Portugal, sailed south along the eastern coast of South America. During these voyages, Vespucci realized that the giant land mass was not Asia, but an extensive new region previously unknown to Europeans. Vespucci wrote an account of his voyages in a pamphlet. In 1507, a German mapmaker named Martin Waldseemüller reprinted the pamphlet with an introduction suggesting that the new lands be named "America," after Vespucci. The name, first applied only to South America, was soon extended to North America.

Life on the Sea

Sailors during the Age of Exploration faced incredible pain, privation, and possibly a watery grave. They could be shipwrecked and starve, be killed by hostile natives, or be slain in battle. Their craft could be hurled into shoreline rocks or swallowed by the stormy sea. They could spend weeks in boredom, the winds dead and the sails hanging listlessly. They endured disease—such as fevers, dysentery, and plagues. Scurvy, which made gums black and puffy, teeth fall out, and limbs weak, killed more sailors than shipwreck. Sailors could look forward to one hot meal a day, usually served around noon. At sea, the sailor's diet was primarily salted pork and a biscuit made from flour, salt, and water. Food stores became infested with worms, mice, and rats, and sailors often complained that food smelled of mouse urine. To relieve their thirst, sailors drank water or wine. The wine became rancid and the water was sometimes so fouled that the crew held their noses while drinking it. Time was marked by an hourglass filled with sand. When one half emptied, usually after about four hours, a boy called out the time and turned the glass over. The sailors switched shifts, one going to work, the other to rest and eat. The sailors had no special place to sleep, and simply picked a spot belowdecks and tried to get as comfortable as possible. This situation changed for the better after the sailors copied how the Indians slept—in hammocks.

searching for a passage through North America to the Indies. He found a giant strait that led west, but winter ice forced him to return to England in early 1509. There, the new king, Henry VIII, showed little enthusiasm for exploration. Frustrated, Cabot went to Spain, where he stayed for the next 30 years. In 1526, he led a Spanish expedition to find a shorter route around the world than the route made by Ferdinand Magellan's sailors, who completed the journey in 1522. But Cabot only got as far as Brazil, where he heard reports of a wealthy kingdom inland. He abandoned his mission and sailed up rivers into Paraguay. He found nothing and returned to Spain, unsuccessful and in disgrace. After his failure, Cabot returned to England and led two more voyages to North America. Again, he failed to find a passage to the Indies. In his last journey, he tried to sail north around Finland to reach Russia. He was forced to

The dreaded disease scurvy was caused by the lack of Vitamin C. In 1795, British sailors were ordered to drink a ration of lime juice a day. The ration cured the disease and gave the sailors a nickname they carry to this day—Limeys.

turn back, but his persistence earned him the title "the elder statesman of the Age of Discovery."

Who was Ferdinand Magellan?

The Portuguese controlled the trade routes around Africa and to India, forcing the Spanish to seek a westward route to the Indies. By the early 1500s, they realized that Columbus had not landed in China or the Spice Islands but on a whole new continent with a vast ocean on the other side. Vainly, they tried to find a river or strait that led through the landmass.

Hoping to discover the western route to the Indies, the Spanish king Charles I approved an expedition led by a Portuguese captain, Ferdinand Magellan. Magellan was born in 1480 in Sabrosa, Portugal. At age 12, Ferdinand was sent to the School of Pages, where he learned music, sword technique, dance, and how to conduct himself in the royal court. The school also taught Ferdinand astronomy, navi-

Ferdinand Magellan is credited as the first man to circumnavigate the world. However, his death in the Philippines during the expedition meant that he never enjoyed the glory of his achievement.

Speed in Knots

In the 1500s, captains began spooling a line of string out the back of the ship as it moved. At intervals, knots were tied into the string. By counting the number of knots that were released in a half-hour, the captain could calculate the speed of the ship. Today, ship speed is still measured in "knots," the length of which has been standardized to about 6,076 feet.

gation, and mathematics. Magellan dreamed of exploring the seas. At age 24, he joined a Portuguese armada as a common sailor. The armada sailed to the Indies, where it attacked Arab traders and ports in an attempt to destroy their role in the spice trade. Magellan's bravery in battle was noticed by his officers. But for a reason not known today, Magellan was hated by King Manuel of Portugal, and his plans for exploration were frustrated. Finally, Magellan traveled to Spain and offered his services. Magellan persuaded King Charles that a western passageway to the Indies existed through South America. Delighted by the chance to extend Spanish rule, King Charles agreed to sponsor Magellan's voyage.

How did Magellan circumnavigate the world?

In September 1519, five ships manned by 250 sailors left Spain to the thunderous salutes of cannon. Magellan's ship took the lead. "Follow my flag by day and my lantern by night," he ordered the other captains. The expedition crossed the Atlantic Ocean and probed the coast of Brazil, searching for a passage. But the coastline, thick with jungle, stretched southward without break. As they continued south, ice formed on the rigging, and the crew began to mutter among themselves that the voyage was doomed. Some men rebelled. Magellan crushed the mutiny and refused to turn back. For six months during the winter (which lasts from May to October in the Southern Hemisphere), the miserable crew huddled together on the southern tip of Argentina. In November 1520, the ships finally rounded the tip of South America and entered a new body of water. Magellan, marveling at the calm waters, called it the Pacific, meaning "peaceful." By this time, only three of the five ships remained. One had been wrecked and the other had fled home.

For the next two months, the three ships sailed across the huge expanse of the Pacific Ocean. Food ran dangerously low and the sailors began to starve and die from disease. Finally, after 97 days, the ships landed on Guam, where the crew eagerly feasted on fresh fruits and meat. On April 27, 1521, Magellan led a party ashore on the Philippines and was ambushed by warriors. As the men scrambled back to the ships, Magellan was struck down and killed. Mourning their fallen leader, the surviving sailors burned one ship and continued on in the remaining two. But one ship began to split apart and was left behind for repairs. The sole surviving ship and crew continued on to Africa, rounded the southern tip of the great continent, and arrived in Spain on September 8, 1522. The Spanish were shocked by the arrival, almost three years after the voyage began. Of the 250 men who began the voyage, only 18 gaunt survivors returned. The Spanish king honored the surviving captain, Juan Sebastian del Cano, as the first man to circumnavigate the globe. But many historians say that Magellan, who had previously voyaged to the Indies, was indeed the first man to circle the globe.

Who was Giovanni da Verrazano?

Giovanni da Verrazano was born about 1485 into an aristocratic family that owned estates south of Florence, Italy. In 1506, Verrazano left his privileged life and moved to Dieppe, France, to learn the ways of the sea. He gained experience on commercial voyages and became a captain of a French war vessel.

In 1524, the French king provided Verrazano with four ships to lead a voyage of exploration to North America. Shortly after leaving France, two ships were wrecked and a third returned to France with riches plundered from Spanish merchant vessels. With 50 sailors aboard *La Dauphine*, Verrazano pushed on, eventually reaching Cape Fear off North Carolina. Verrazano, like most explorers, was searching for a water route through North America. Long, narrow sandbars run along the North Carolina coast. Verrazano looked at these sandbars and saw the sea behind them. He

The caravel, with its triangular main sail, was a small, fast, and seaworthy ship used by many European captains in the 1400s. Columbus and da Gama made their voyages in caravels.

The Ships

Ship design improved greatly in the late 1200s, 1300s, and 1400s, eventually allowing sailors to venture into turbulent oceans and survive journeys of several years. The advances came from combining two kinds of ships—those used in the Mediterranean and those used by the Vikings. In their original form, both ships were pulled by one sail and steered with a rudder off one side. In the north, shipbuilders greatly improved steering by placing the rudder in the rear. In the Mediterranean, ships were built larger and two sails were added for more power. In the 1400s, shipbuilders combined the two designs into a durable, fast vessel that could be easily maneuvered.

The first European explorers sailed in a ship called the caravel. Two main masts supported triangle-shaped sails, with a smaller one in the rear. It was a narrow ship, allowing it to slice through ocean waves. But it also had a shallow keel, allowing captains to sail close to shore. The deck was sealed with caulked planks, allowing waves to spill over and drain without swamping the lower compartments. Da Gama sailed a caravel around Africa, and Columbus led three caravels on his first journey to North America. As voyages grew longer and more stores were needed, a bigger ship called the nao was built. The nao had three large masts supporting square sails with a triangular one in the rear. Magellan's five ships were all naos.

did not see the mainland of the giant continent, and he assumed that the water was the Pacific Ocean, meaning he had found the sea route. Fearing the hostile Spanish to the south, Verrazano sailed north. He encountered several American Indians, whom he described as "well fashioned" and "well favored." On April 17, 1525, Verrazano entered a broad channel leading to a well-protected harbor. Today the strait—the entrance to New York City—is named after Verrazano. Verrazano continued north to Massachusetts and Maine. There, he encountered Indians—Abnaki—who shot arrows at the French. In disgust, he named the area "Land of the Bad People." When he reached Newfoundland, Verrazano turned east and returned to France. Verrazano made two more voyages, one to Brazil and another to Florida and the Leeward Islands. After landing at one, probably Guadeloupe, Verrazano was seized, killed, and reportedly eaten by cannibals.

Who were the conquistadors?

During the 1500s, Spanish explorers, called conquistadors, plundered the native Indian civilizations of North and South America of their gold and silver and enslaved the inhabitants. They were brave, hard, and ruthless men who were quick to use their swords, having honed their skills during years of fighting Muslims in Spain. The conquistadors put millions of Indians under Spanish rule. Ships, heavily loaded with bars of gold and silver, sailed back to Spain, making it the richest nation on earth. The Spanish Empire would endure 300 years.

Who was Vasco Núñez de Balboa?

Balboa was a daring conquistador who discovered and claimed the Pacific Ocean for Spain in 1513. Born in 1475, Balboa grew up in a family of low-ranking nobility. In 1501, he left Spain and traveled to Hispaniola (Haiti and Dominican Republic today) to make his fortune. He ran a plantation and tried to raise hogs, but he fell into debt and fled his creditors by hiding in a cask aboard a supply ship. Bound for the Spanish colony San Sebastián, today in Colombia, the ship was wrecked and the crew later rescued by another famous Spanish conquistador,

Francisco Pizarro. When the crew learned that San Sebastián had been destroyed by an Indian attack, Balboa convinced his shipmates to sail on to Panama, a more peaceful area. They agreed, and Balboa and his companions established a settlement at Darien.

Local Indian stories told of a rich empire to the south and a vast "South Sea." When Balboa asked the Spanish king Ferdinand II for an army to find and conquer this empire, Ferdinand agreed. But he appointed someone else as commander. Furious, in September 1513 Balboa led his own force of about 190 Spaniards into the jungles of Panama in search of the empire and "South Sea." After several weeks of travel through swamps and jungles, Balboa reached a mountain plateau and gazed south. Stretching to the horizon was the vast Pacific Ocean. On that day, September 25, Balboa held a thanksgiving service and claimed the surrounding lands for Spain. The expedition reached the beach and Balboa waded into the waters with the Spanish flag, claiming the entire body of water for Spain. Balboa returned to Darien, only to find that a governor from Spain had taken control. Balboa and the new governor waged a long, jealous feud for power. Balboa led another expedition to the Pacific in 1517 and explored the Gulf of San Miguel. But in 1519, the governor had Balboa beheaded for treason.

Who searched for the Fountain of Youth?

American Indians told the Spanish on Hispaniola about a magical fountain on islands to the west. Whoever drank the fountain's waters, they said, would become young again. A Spanish conquistador named Juan Ponce de León heard the miraculous story and in 1513 launched an expedition to find it. De León was an experienced explorer. In 1493, he reportedly accompanied Columbus on his second expedition to the Americas and became governor of the western half of Hispaniola. In 1508, he colonized Puerto Rico.

On March 27, 1513, de León spotted a lush, green land on the western horizon. The Spanish landed—the first Spanish to set foot on North America. Since the date fell on Easter (called *Pascua Florida* in Spanish) and the vegetation was so beautiful, de León named the region "Tierra La Florida"—"land of the flowers." The Spanish spent the next five months sailing down Florida's eastern coast, around the key islands, and north again along the west coast. Florida, de León realized, was a giant peninsula. When de León returned to Spain in 1514, he was knighted by the king and given permission to colonize Florida. De León returned to Florida in 1521, where he and his men were attacked by Seminole Indians. De León was wounded by an arrow, and the Spanish withdrew to Havana, Cuba. De León died of the wound in July 1521. De León never discovered the mythical Fountain of Youth, but he spread Spain's claims in North America.

How did Cortés encounter the Aztecs?

Hernán Cortés was born in Spain in 1485, and he grew up in a family with "little wealth, but much honor." Like many other Spanish noblemen, Cortés looked to the Americas for adventure and riches. At age 19, he sailed for Hispaniola. Over the next decade, Cortés took part in the conquest of Cuba and gained political power. In February 1519, Cortés led 11 ships loaded with more than 500 soldiers and 16 horses on an expedition to the coast of Mexico. Cortés had heard rumors of fabulous riches in the unknown land, and he dreamed of finding gold and silver and returning to Spain in triumph. In March, the expedition landed on what is now the Yucatán Peninsula in Mexico and fought a battle with Indians. The Indian warriors fought bravely to repel the invaders, but they were no match for Spanish swords and guns. When the Spanish cavalry attacked, the Indians, who had never seen horses before, believed horse and rider were actually a single beast. They fled in terror.

News of the Spanish victory spread through the country, finally reaching Montezuma, ruler of the Aztec Empire. The Aztec Empire covered most of what is now Mexico. In the magnificent capital city of Tenochtitlan, Montezuma pondered the significance of the white men's arrival. A religious prophecy declared that an Aztec god, Quetzalcóatl, would return as a bearded, fair-skinned man in the year 1519. But Montezuma remained uncertain

whether the white men should be slaughtered as invaders or welcomed as gods. Montezuma sent them magnificent gifts—two large gold and silver disks, pearl and turquoise ornaments, and jeweled robes. Cortés was delighted by these signs of wealth. He saw these gifts as confirmation of the Aztec Empire's incredible riches, and he resolved to win them for himself.

An Aztec artist drew this picture of Cortés approaching a group of Aztec leaders. Cortés's first meetings with the Aztecs were relatively peaceful. Later, Cortés and his men would violently conquer the Aztec empire.

How did Cortés conquer the Aztecs?

In July 1519, Cortés deliberately burned and sank, or scuttled, his ten ships. Cortés knew that the impending campaign would be difficult, and he didn't want any of his men to mutiny and try to flee on their own. His message sent, Cortés led an army of 1,000 Spanish and Indian allies into the mountains and jungles. As Cortés's army defeated Indian warriors and sacked several towns, Montezuma sent gifts, promising to pay tribute if the Spanish left the Aztec Empire. Cortés defied the emperor and by November, Cortés and his ragged army stood before the gates of Tenochtitlan, the Aztec capital and home to more than 60,000 people, a population larger than that in any Spanish city at the time. At first, Montezuma and Cortés exchanged cordial greetings. Cortés and his men were stunned by the magnificence of the city, but they were also horrified by the Aztec religion, which sacrificed humans in rituals. When one of

Montezuma's chiefs attacked a Spanish garrison, Cortés took Montezuma prisoner and forced him to acknowledge the Spanish king as his lord. When Cortés tried to change the Aztec temples into Christian churches, warfare broke out. Montezuma was killed, and Cortés and his men were forced to flee Tenochtitlan. Cortés raised an army and returned to lay siege to the great city. On August 13, 1521, the Aztecs, starving and weakened by disease introduced by the Europeans, surrendered. Cortés was made governor and captain general of Nuevo España (New Spain), and established Mexico City on the ruins of Tenochtitlan.

The Incan Empire, with more than 16 million people, was crisscrossed with an elaborate network of paved roads. Its artists produced exquisite works in gold and silver.

How did Pizarro conquer the Incans?

Little is known about the Spanish conquistador Francisco Pizarro before he arrived in Hispaniola in 1502. He joined an expedition into Colombia and earned the reputation as a quiet, brave fighter. In 1519, he became the mayor of Panama and made a small fortune. He stayed for several years before deciding to take a bold gamble.

In autumn 1532, Pizarro set off with 106 infantry and 62 cavalry into the peaks of the Andes mountains to conquer the Incan Empire of South America. The Incan emperor, Atahualpa, learned of the Spanish party and sent a note welcoming them, but he did not plan to let the Spanish stay. When the Spanish arrived in the Incan city of Cajamarca, they found it deserted. Atahualpa, encamped with a giant army, waited nearby. Pizarro and Atahualpa exchanged greetings again, and Atahualpa promised to meet the Spaniard in the town square the next day. When Atahualpa arrived with 6,000 warriors, the Spanish soldiers waited in ambush. Suddenly, they swarmed out of their hiding places and began slaughtering the surprised warriors. Terrified by the horses, the Indians were routed, leaving more than 2,000 dead. Atahualpa was taken prisoner and Pizarro demanded a room filled with gold and two chambers filled with silver in ransom. To save their king, Incans across the empire tore gold and silver from their temples and their homes and sent it to Pizarro. In May 1533, Pizarro's men built nine forges to melt the metal into bars. Thousands of priceless artworks were lost. When the Spanish finished, they counted 13,265 pounds of gold and 26,000 pounds of silver. Realizing that a free Atahualpa could rally his people, Pizarro ordered him executed by strangulation in August 1533. With his death, the Incan Empire fell under Spanish control.

Who was Hernando de Soto?

Around 1500, Hernando de Soto was born to a family who intended him for a career in law. But all of Spain spoke of the discoveries, adventures, and conquests in South America, and de Soto decided to become a conquistador instead. As a teenager, de Soto trained with Spanish captains in Latin America, where he learned the arts of war. He traveled in the advance guard of Pizarro's army when it entered South America and conquered the Incans. De Soto returned to Spain, wealthy and honored, but his desire for glory was still unsatisfied. In May 1539, de Soto led ten ships filled with 1,000 men and 350 horses from Havana, Cuba, on an expedition to conquer the territory of La Florida in North America. De Soto hoped to discover a civilization as rich and powerful as those of the Aztecs and Incans.

After almost two weeks at sea, de Soto and his men landed near what is now Tampa, on the western side of the Florida peninsula. They built a base and moved north. If any Indians acted unfriendly, de Soto destroyed their village and either massacred or enslaved the inhabitants. The Indians told de Soto of a rich, gold-filled empire to the north called Cofitachequi. The Spanish marched northeast into present-day Georgia and Tennessee. Still, the men discovered no gold. Local Indians, however, hoping to get rid of the Spanish as soon as possible, insisted that the wealthy empire they sought was nearby. The expedition moved into Alabama and northern Mississippi. On May 8, 1541, the expedition reached the Mississippi River, becoming the first Europeans to see the great river. By then, de Soto's men were exhausted and low on both food and ammunition. They traveled, during a brutal summer drought, down to Arkansas. After winter, the Spanish traveled into Louisiana. There, de Soto fell ill with a fever and died on May 21, 1542. The men weighted his body with stones and sank him in a river, so the local Indians would not discover his death. The survivors built boats and sailed into the Gulf of Mexico, finally reaching Spanish colonists in Tampico, Mexico, in September 1543. They had traveled more than 4,000 miles.

Who searched for the Seven Cities of Gold?

News of the astounding wealth in South America fired the ambition of other Spanish explorers. Rumors told of seven cities that shimmered with gold to the north of Mexico in a legendary land called Cíbola. In February 1540, Spanish nobleman Francisco Vásquez de Coronado led an expedition of 336 soldiers and 1,300 Indians northward out of Mexico and into what is today the American Southwest. Guided by a priest named Fray Marcos, the Spanish traveled slowly through the deserts in Arizona. In June, the half-starved Spanish army reached Háwikuh, an Indian city in what is now New Mexico. But instead of a dazzling city of gold, the Spanish found squat structures built from adobe clay. Worse, the Indians did not welcome the Spanish, but instead shot arrows and hurled stones at their approach. Coronado was knocked unconscious before the Spanish soldiers seized the village and eagerly feasted on the corn and chickens they found there. The Spanish soon learned that the Seven Cities of Cíbola did not exist. Disgusted, Coronado sent Marcos home in disgrace.

How did Coronado continue his exploration?

After listening to Indian tales of a great river, Coronado ordered a search party to travel northwest of Háwikuh. They did but were halted by a massive canyon—the Grand Canyon. The Colorado River flowed at its distant bottom. The following spring, Coronado and the army set off again, this time toward the east, where rumor told of gold. The men marched across the dusty plains of Texas and Kansas, stunned by the enormous buffalo herds, but they found only cities of huts and buffalo hides. Coronado was shocked to learn that his Indian guide had deliberately led the Spanish into the Plains in the hopes that they would die of hunger and thirst. Coronado had the man executed immediately. In the spring of 1542, Coronado and his weary men returned to Mexico, with nothing to show after two years of exploration.

Who was Estévanico?

In the early 1500s, Estévanico, a Moor, was captured in his homeland of Morocco and sold as a slave in Spain. He became the servant of Andrés Dorantes, who commanded a company of Spanish infantry. In 1528, Dorantes and his men joined an expedition to Florida led by Pánfilo de Narváez. About 400 men and 42 horses survived the trip to Florida. Estévanico was among them. Narváez led the party into the interior in search of gold but found little. Instead, they traveled through swampy terrain and began to die of disease. Near Tallahassee, the group was attacked by Seminole Indians. By September, the weak and hungry men decided to build five rafts and attempt to sail from Florida to a Spanish settlement in Mexico. The voyage was a disaster. Some rafts were shattered on the coast. Another, with Narváez aboard, was pulled out to sea and never seen again. Two rafts, including the one occupied by Estévanico, were shipwrecked near what is now Galveston, Texas. By spring 1529, only 15 men still lived.

The group decided to cross Texas to the safety of Mexico. They were captured by Indians and spent the next six years enduring harsh treatment and labor. At the end of 1535, Estévanico and three companions escaped. As they traveled west through Texas, their strange appearance caused Indians to believe that they possessed magical healing powers. Word of the healers spread rapidly, making their journey much less dangerous. They reached Mexico City in July 1536. Because of his experience and ability to speak several Indian languages, Estévanico became a guide for Coronado's expedition. Estévanico traveled several days ahead of the main party and, as he had done in Texas, offered his healing powers. In May 1537, Estévanico reached the Zuni pueblo of Háwikuh. There, the chief was not impressed by Estévanico's claim to be a medicine man. The chief forced Estévanico to leave the village and the next day ambushed him with a group of warriors, killing him.

The Spanish explorers introduced the Indians to an animal unknown in North and South America—the horse. Life for the Plains Indians changed forever. Hunting buffalo and traveling became easier, allowing the Plains Indians to prosper. Two hundred years after Coronado's exploration, white settlers from the eastern United States would describe the Plains Indians as expert horsemen.

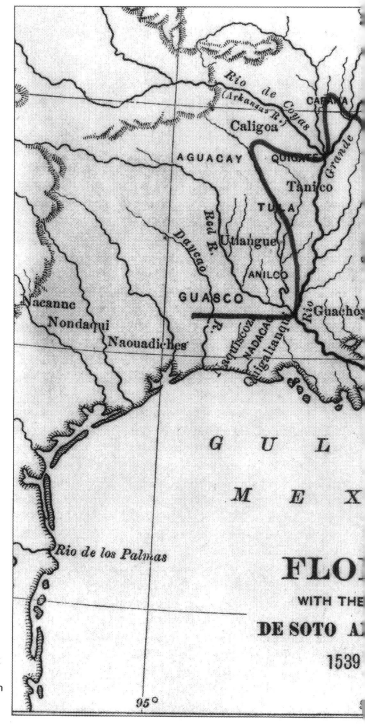

Hernando de Soto's 1539-1543 travels through North America are clearly marked on this 1898 map. De Soto's 4,000-mile march was grueling to his men and disastrous to the Indians they encountered, but it helped enable the Spanish Empire to gain control of the area.

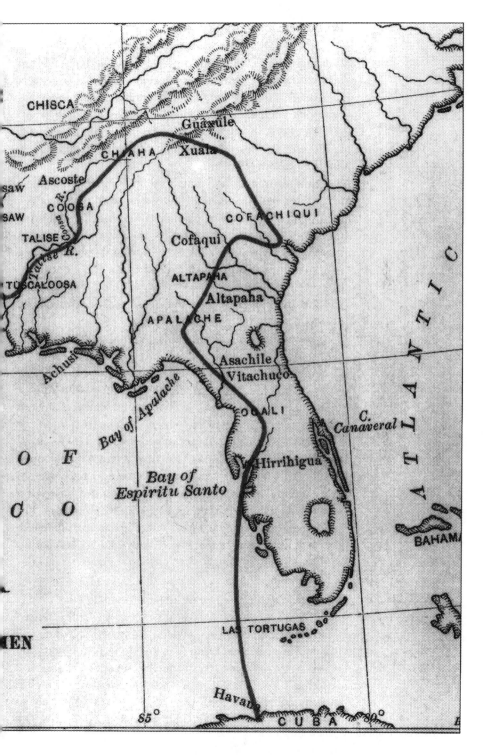

Who was Sir Francis Drake?

Francis Drake was born about 1540 in Devonshire, England. He grew up in poverty, living in the hull of a ship moored in the Thames River. At age 13, Drake became a seaman's apprentice on a ship that traded among the North Sea ports. At age 23, now skilled in seafaring, Drake joined an expedition to the West Indies. His bravery and superb seamanship were noticed by his superiors, including the English queen Elizabeth I.

At the time, Spain and England were competing for power in Europe, and the queen authorized Drake to attack and plunder Spanish shipping.The Spanish transported spices and cloths of the East Indies across the Pacific Ocean to Latin America. Spanish warehouses in Panama brimmed with the riches of trade and conquest. Gold and silver were collected and loaded onto galleons for the slow journey across the Atlantic Ocean to Spain.

Drawn by the tempting targets, Drake led five ships across the Atlantic and down the coast of South America in December 1577. Drake executed one man for conspiring to mutiny and was forced to scuttle two vessels. In August 1578, the remaining ships entered the treacherous strait at the tip of South America, which had been named for Magellan. The English sailors shivered in the bitter cold as Drake carefully maneuvered the fleet through the channel. Finally, in September, Drake and his men joyfully entered the Pacific Ocean. But a storm pounded the fleet soon afterward, and one ship vanished with all its sailors. Just one week later, the remaining two ships were separated. Drake and his crew aboard the *Golden Hind* continued up the coast of Chile alone.

How did Drake circumnavigate the world?

Off the west coast of South America, Drake raided Spanish ships and ports, seizing silver, gold, wine, and jewels. He continued north as far as what is now Oregon, where he was forced to halt due to "most vile, thick, and stinking fogs." Drake now faced a dilemma. His ship already overflowed with plunder, so he dared not try to sail through the hostile and alert Spanish in the south. The only way to return to England, he boldly decided, was to follow Magellan's route across the Pacific. For the next 68 days, the *Golden Hind* sailed west, steadily slicing through the waves of the Pacific Ocean. Finally, the ship stopped at several islands that dot the giant ocean. On one, the natives took whatever they could grab. Drake called the place "Island of Thieves." At the Spice Islands, Drake loaded more valuable cargo before sailing across the Indian Ocean, around the tip of Africa, and north to England. After two years and ten months at sea, Drake and the crew of the *Golden Hind* returned safely to England. The Spanish king, furious with Drake, ordered Queen Elizabeth I to cut off Drake's head. Instead, Elizabeth knighted him, and he became a hero.

What was the Northwest Passage?

The northern European countries—England, Holland, and France—watched the Spanish and the Portuguese grow wealthy from trade with a mixture of envy and resentment. Unable to challenge the Spanish in the southern Atlantic, the northern European explorers searched to the west and north for a sea route to the Indies. They were blocked by a giant landmass—North America. But the French and English were convinced that a channel ran through the continent to the Pacific Ocean and the Spice Islands. Whoever discovered this channel, called the "Northwest Passage," would grow rich from trade. Today,

Crime and Punishment

The worst crime on the high seas was mutiny, and punishment was usually swift and harsh—death. But sailors were not always obedient to their captains, and captains used a variety of punishments to enforce their will. Extra duty or flogging by whips was common, the number of lashes depending on the severity of the crime. In extreme instances, a sailor was "keel-hauled." A sailor was lowered by rope down the bow of the moving ship. Caught in the water, the sailor was dragged under the ship, banging and scraping against the barnacle-encrusted hull. The unfortunate sailor was pulled up from the stern and returned, possibly more repentant, to his duties.

we know that a usable such passage doesn't exist. But the explorers would brave the frigid waters of the North Atlantic to find it. Their attempts failed, but their exploration of the coast of North America opened it to European settlement.

Who was Henry Hudson?

English navigator Henry Hudson was obsessed with discovering the Northwest Passage. Between 1607 and 1611, he sailed farther north than any other European explorer, venturing to the top of the world and braving the icy arctic waters for a passage that did not exist. In his first voyage, Hudson sailed toward Greenland and was blocked by ice. The next year, Hudson tried again, this time sailing along the coast of Norway in an effort to sail around Asia. Again, he was forced to turn back. After two failures, Hudson lost support in England but he found financial backing from Dutch merchants.

In April 1609, Hudson and a 16-man crew set sail in the *Half Moon*. Hudson sailed up the coast of Norway. Temperatures plummeted and ice coated the rigging. The crew refused to go farther. Hudson gave in, but instead of returning to Holland, he ordered the ship westward toward North America. By mid-July, Hudson sighted the coast of Maine. The *Half Moon* made its way down the coast to Virginia and returned north. On September 2, Hudson discovered a giant, beautiful bay at the mouth of a vast river. Excited that this river might be the Northwest Passage, Hudson and the crew sailed north. Indians spotted the giant ship and paddled canoes out to greet it. The Indians "seemed very glad at our coming . . . and are very civil," noted a sailor

The Northwest Passage Exists

Beginning in 1903, the Norwegian explorer Roald Amundsen took three years to navigate through the islands and ice of northern Canada. He was the first to complete a voyage from the Atlantic to the Pacific Ocean through the "Northwest Passage." In 1969, the U.S. ship *Manhattan* sailed the same area by smashing through 650 miles of ice. The route, however, was and remains too difficult to be commercially successful.

Despite appeals, Henry Hudson and several crewmen are set adrift in the frigid waters of Hudson Bay. They were never heard from again.

in a diary, "we durst not trust them." Hudson continued 150 miles before realizing that the river had grown too shallow and narrow to be the passage. Disappointed, Hudson left the river that to this day bears his name. The Dutch claimed the Hudson River Valley and founded a city called New Amsterdam, known today as New York.

How did Hudson's explorations end?

After Hudson returned to Europe, he reasoned that the Northwest Passage must exist farther north. In April 1610, Hudson received English support and led another ship, the *Discovery*, into the North Atlantic. He rounded the tip of

Greenland and made his way along the northern coast of Canada. Picking his way through fog and sheets of ice, Hudson sailed into a giant bay. He was jubilant. Here was a sea that seemed to stretch all the way to the Pacific. But the bay ended in the frigid Canadian wilderness. With the landscape locked in snow and ice, Hudson ordered the crew to wait out the winter. Blasted by the arctic cold and depressed by the long nights, the crew spent six miserable months on the desolate shores of what became known as Hudson Bay. Rations dwindled and the men faced starvation. In June 1611, the crew mutinied. Hudson, his son, and seven sailors were forced into a small boat and set adrift into the bleak waters of Hudson Bay. They were never seen again. The *Discovery* returned to England, where the leaders of the mutiny were punished.

Who was Jacques Cartier?

French explorers also sailed across the North Atlantic in the vain hope of finding the Northwest Passage. Fishermen of Portugal and France, who had followed schools of codfish into the North Atlantic, found great bays and inlets along the coast of North America. Hoping one of them might lead to the Northwest Passage, French explorer Jacques Cartier led two ships into the Gulf of St. Lawrence in 1534. From the gulf, the giant St. Lawrence River disappeared into the interior of North America. Surely, thought

Souls and Fur

In the 1600s and 1700s, furs from North America were in great demand in Europe. Beaver pelts were used in men's hats, and fur trading became a highly profitable industry. As the Spanish had been drawn south, the lure of riches—this time in the fur trade—drew young Frenchmen to brave the wilderness of North America.

While many were motivated by greed, others wished to save souls. Beginning in 1611, French Catholic Jesuit priests ventured deep into North America, building churches and converting Indian tribes to Christianity. Many suffered incredible privation, torture, and death for their faith. These twin motives—profit and souls—drove the early exploration of French North America.

Cartier, this was the passage. He returned two years later, sailed up the St. Lawrence River, and was halted at impassable rapids. Still hopeful that he would eventually break through to the Indies, he named the rapids *La Chine*, or China.

Who was Samuel de Champlain?

Champlain, a Frenchman, gained experience in navigation on voyages to the West Indies and Central America in the late 1500s. Champlain's skill drew the notice of the French king Henry IV. Invited by the king, Champlain accompanied a French expedition up the St. Lawrence River in North America in 1603. In 1608, Champlain returned and founded a trading post called Quebec. Using the post as his base, Champlain traveled on foot and by canoe into the mountains to the south, gazing upon the giant lake in northern New York that bears his name today—Lake Champlain. In 1615, Champlain traveled through the rugged forests to the west and paddled across the first of the Great Lakes, Lake Ontario. Champlain's routes were followed by French trappers eager to trade with Indians. As a result, French settlements gradually grew in Canada.

Who was La Salle? ◆ How did La Salle claim the
Mississippi River? ◆ Did La Salle bring French settlers
to Louisiana? ◆ Who was Alexander Mackenzie? ◆
How did   Who were
Lewis and Clark? ◆ Who was Sacajawea? ◆ How did
the expedition reach the Pacific Ocean? ◆ How did
the Lewis and Clark   Who was John
Charles Frémont? ◆ Who was Alexander von Humboldt?
◆ Who was Wilhelm Ludwig Le
eichhardt? ◆ Who were Burke and Wills? ◆ How did
the Wills and Burke expedition end in tragedy? ◆
Who was Mungo Park? ◆ Who was Heinrich Barth?

EXPLORING GRAND CONTINENTS

Who was La Salle?

Robert Cavalier, Sieur de La Salle, was born in 1643 and studied in Jesuit schools to become a priest. But lured by the opportunity of adventure and fortune in North America, the 22-year-old Frenchman traveled to Montreal, a city on the banks of the St. Lawrence River. He cleared a patch of nearby forest and set up a fur post to trade with local Indians, including the Hurons and Ottawas. Although his business thrived, the young La Salle grew restless. He heard stories that described a giant waterway to the west, a river that sliced through the dense North American forest. Hoping that the river led to the Pacific Ocean, La Salle sold his trading post and organized an expedition to find it. He assembled woodsmen, Indian guides, and missionaries in eight canoes and led them down the St. Lawrence River in 1669. The expedition paddled into Lake Ontario and found the Ohio River to the south. The river flowed steadily to the southwest, and La Salle was excited thinking it might be the Northwest Passage. But after several months, the expedition was halted by a stretch of roaring rapids. Frustrated, La Salle turned back and returned to Montreal.

How did La Salle claim the Mississippi River?

In 1673, La Salle learned that two Frenchmen, Louis Jolliet and Father Jacques Marquette, had paddled down what Indians called the Father of Waters—the Mississippi River. They had not reached the Gulf of Mexico but had turned back at the mouth of the Arkansas River. La Salle was disappointed to learn that the Mississippi did not reach the Pacific Ocean, but he realized the economic potential of the great waterway. In 1677, he went to France and told King Louis XIV of the splendid, untamed country and its promise of riches beyond their dreams. The king, inspired by La Salle's vision of a French empire, granted him a monopoly to build trading posts and forts in the Mississippi Valley. In February 1682, La Salle led an expedition of 23 Frenchmen and 31 Indians—including members of the Illinois, Miami, Shawnee, and Abnaki tribes—down the Mississippi River. Along the way, La Salle shrewdly negotiated with Indians, using gifts and flattering language to convince them of his friendly intentions. Still, he claimed their land for Louis XIV, erecting wooden crosses with the arms of France and crying, *"Vive le Roi!"* On April 6, 1682, La Salle arrived at the Gulf of Mexico and claimed the entire Mississippi River and its tributaries. He named the colony Louisiana, after the king. In one journey, La Salle had created a French colony several times larger in area than the French nation.

Did La Salle bring French settlers to Louisiana?

Hoping to attract French colonists, La Salle returned to France, recruited 280 settlers, and set sail again for Louisiana in 1684. The voyage was disastrous. The ships mistakenly sailed past the mouth of the Mississippi River and La Salle was forced to send the settlers ashore on the barren coast of Texas. One ship was wrecked; another returned home. La Salle set off with a band of 20 men eastward across the harsh Texas landscape in a desperate bid to find the river. But food ran out, frustration rose, and tempers shortened. Finally, some of the men revolted and shot La Salle at point blank range, leaving his body to be eaten by vultures.

Who was Alexander Mackenzie?

Born in Scotland around 1755, Alexander Mackenzie left his native country for Canada in 1779. He settled in

Alexander Mackenzie, the leader of the first exploratory expeditions into western and northern Canada, was determined to reach the Pacific Ocean. His first journey ended in failure on the Arctic Ocean. The second arrived at the Pacific in 1793, ten years before the American explorers Lewis and Clark began their expedition west.

Montreal, which had grown into a flourishing city, and joined the fur-trading business. Nine years later, Mackenzie moved westward into the Canadian wilderness, where he established a trading post on the shore of Lake Athabasca in northern Alberta. Indian traders told him that the Pacific Ocean existed to the west. Some said that it was quite near. Like so many other explorers at that time, Mackenzie dreamed of finding a water route across North America that linked the Atlantic and Pacific oceans. In June 1789, he led an expedition in three birchbark canoes northward to a giant body of water called Great Slave Lake. The party discovered a river at the lake's western end that flowed west. Eagerly, Mackenzie and his companions followed the river west and then north. The trees grew stockier, the wildlife more rare. After 11 days, the explorers entered a vast, icy, treeless region covered with rocks and lichen. Mackenzie

continued on page 56

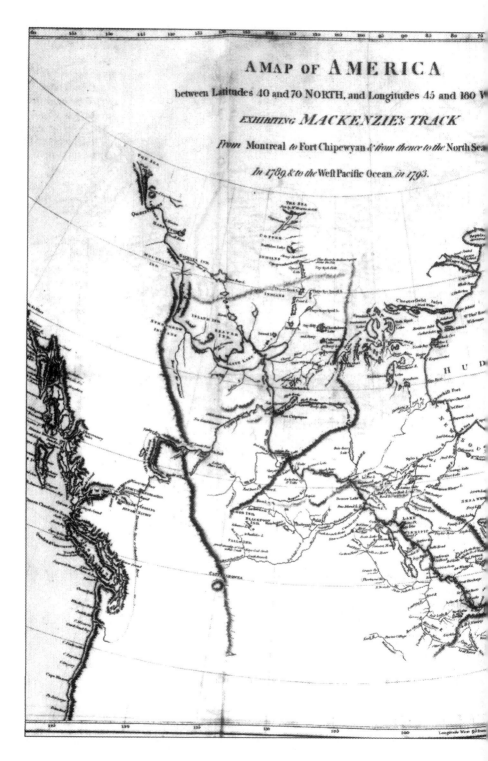

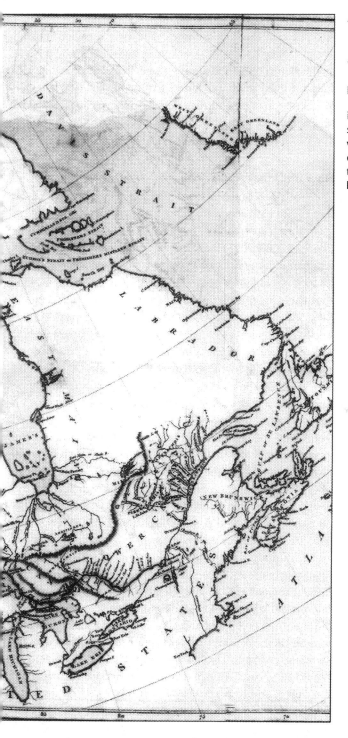

Alexander Mackenzie's map of northwestern North America, drawn after his 1789 and 1793 expeditions, was published in his book *Voyages from Montreal* in 1801. The map shows the numerous waterways Mackenzie explored, including the river that now bears his name.

continued from page 53

had reached the Arctic tundra. The river emptied into an ocean clogged with ice. Mackenzie had discovered a route to the ocean, but to the wrong one. Instead of gazing joyfully on the Pacific, he stared glumly at the Arctic Ocean. Mackenzie named the river Disappointment and returned to his trading post, having traveled nearly 3,000 miles. Today, Disappointment River is called the Mackenzie River.

How did Mackenzie reach the Pacific?

Frustrated but undaunted, Mackenzie vowed to reach the Pacific. After spending a year in England studying astronomy, navigation, and geography, he led another expedition into the Canadian wilderness in May 1793. The ten-man party and its equipment were loaded into a single 25-foot birchbark canoe. The canoe, sturdy but light, carried the group as it swiftly paddled west up the Peace River. After two weeks, Mackenzie spotted the peaks of the Rocky Mountains in the distance. The river narrowed and entered chasms, accelerating the current and crashing the water into white foam over treacherous rocks. Abandoning their paddles, the men struggled to pole and pull the canoe upriver. The water often caught the canoe and smashed it against rocks, tearing holes in its hull. The men stopped frequently for repairs, and some wondered whether the journey was doomed to failure. But Mackenzie refused to give up. He ordered the men to carry the canoe and its supplies overland, an agonizing journey through forests and fields thick with underbrush. After three days the exhausted party had traveled past the rapids and was able to navigate the Peace River again.

For another three weeks, the group struggled west, finally meeting an Indian who guided them to a river that flowed toward the Pacific. But the trip downstream was often more difficult than paddling upstream. At one point the men lost control of the canoe, running into rocks that tore off the bow and stern and spilled the supplies into the swirling current. The men thought certainly that they would turn back. But Mackenzie ordered them to repair the canoe, and they continued. On July 20, 1793, the party finally spilled out of a river into a salty bay just north of

Vancouver Island. After ten weeks of grueling travel, Mackenzie had reached the Pacific. He took navigational readings and guided the party home. In 1801, he published an account of his travels in *Voyages from Montreal*. One of the most enthusiastic readers of the book was an American president named Thomas Jefferson.

Who were Lewis and Clark?

In 1803, President Thomas Jefferson made one of the greatest land purchases in history. The French emperor Napoléon, in need of money to finance his military operations in Europe, offered to sell all French territory in North America for $15 million, or 3 cents an acre. The Louisiana Purchase, which included the entire Mississippi River and its tributary rivers and streams, doubled the size of the United States. Jefferson, always curious about science and nature, wanted to know more about this largely unexplored territory. What was the landscape? What animals and plants lived there? What kind of people inhabited the land and how did they live? To answer these questions, Jefferson organized an expedition and chose a close friend—29-year-old Meriwether Lewis—to lead it. Lewis realized the importance and danger of the journey. He invited another friend, William Clark, to share command. These two explorers, Lewis and Clark, would spend more than two years and travel 8,000 miles in the most famous exploratory journey in U.S. history.

Who was Sacajawea?

During the winter of 1803–1804, Lewis and Clark camped at the spot where the Missouri River joins the Mississippi. The expedition included 29 soldiers and 16 helpers who would accompany them for the first year before turning back. The men, food, and equipment would travel in two dugout canoes and a 55-foot boat. On May 14, 1804, the expedition began to paddle and row up the Missouri River. For weeks, the men made their way up the broad river, avoiding floating logs, snags, and shifting sands. By mid-July, they had reached the broad, grass-covered land of the Great Plains, which stretched unbroken to the horizon. Over the next two months, Lewis wrote fascinating accounts of the local animal life—including

continued on page 60

The Lewis and Clark expedition traveled on its stomach. In order to feed his 45 men for 24 hours, Lewis wrote that it required either four deer, an elk and a deer, or one buffalo.

This 1797 map is one of seven published in *The American Gazetteer*, the first comprehensive geography of North America. Created by clergyman, educator, and geographer Jedediah Morse (the father of Samuel Morse, inventor of the telegraph), the map shows the imaginary "River of the West" and vast areas of blankness west of the Mississippi, revealing the extent of knowledge at the time.

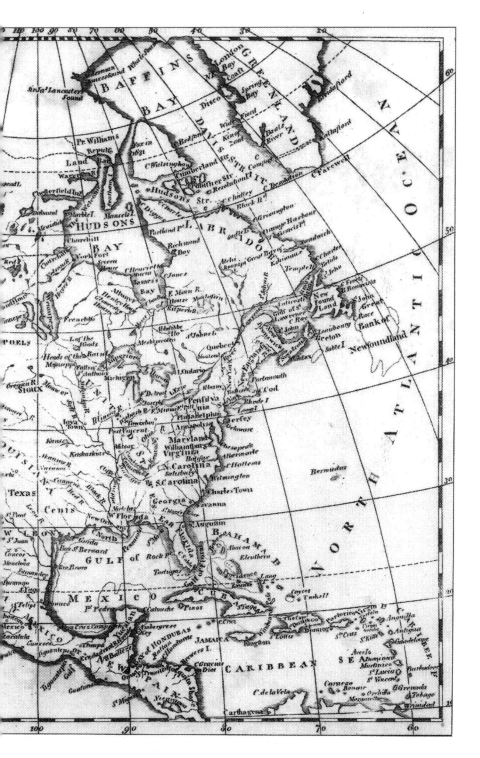

Meriwether Lewis, standing gracefully with his musket, led with William Clark the most famous exploratory mission in U.S. history into the unmapped regions of the American West and Northwest.

continued from page 57

antelopes, badgers, jackrabbits, and coyotes. Herds of buffalo darkened the plains. Little animals lived by the hundreds in underground burrows. Their high-pitched squeals and calls echoed for miles. Lewis called them "barking squirrels." A sergeant called them prairie dogs, the name they have today.

By November, the expedition had traveled 1,600 miles. As the weather turned cold, the men began to build a camp on the banks of the Missouri to wait out the winter. Before they finished, a French-Canadian fur trader, Toussaint Charbonneau, offered to join the expedition and act as an interpreter. Lewis was more impressed with Charbonneau's wife, a young Indian woman named Sacajawea. She was Shoshone, a tribe that lived in the foothills of the Rocky Mountains, where Lewis expected to travel. They persuaded Sacajawea to come with them. In the coming months, Sacajawea would be invaluable to the expedition, and not just because of her translating skills. In February, Sacajawea gave birth to a son. When the expedition met Indian tribes for the first time, the presence of Sacajawea, with her baby strapped securely to her back, calmed the chiefs. No party with a woman and child intended to make war.

"Sacajawea's presence," wrote Clark, "reconciles all the Indians as to our friendly intentions."

How did the expedition arrive at the Pacific Ocean?

In April 1805, the expedition's boat, a canoe, and 12 men returned to St. Louis loaded with reports, maps, dried plants, animal skins, Indian artifacts, and crates of other material collected by the explorers. Lewis and Clark and the rest of the men continued west. Lewis was astounded at the size, strength, and ferocity of the grizzly bear, which often required several shots to be killed. "I had rather fight two Indians than one bear," he observed. By late May, the expedition had traveled more than 2,000 miles, and some of the men wondered whether the Missouri River would ever end. But on May 26, Lewis glimpsed the snowy peaks of the Rocky Mountains in the distance. After another two months, the expedition reached the headwaters of the Missouri River, country inhabited by the Shoshone. But the men found only empty, abandoned Indian camps. The Shoshone, apparently terrified by the visitors, had gone into hiding. Finally, Lewis surprised three Indian women and convinced them he was friendly. When the Shoshone chief, Cameahwait, arrived at the white man's camp,

Sacajawea burst into tears and embraced him. The chief was her brother. When the expedition left the Shoshone in late August, the tribe provided it with 29 horses and a new guide named Toby, though Sacajawea continued to travel with the expedition.

For three weeks in September 1805, the party struggled through the Bitterroot Mountains. The terrain was treacherous with thick forest covering steep, rocky slopes. Food supplies ran desperately low. Worse, snow came down in sheets, making the party miserable. Clark recalled being "wet and as cold in every part as I ever was in my life." They finally reached a Nez Percé Indian village, where the expedition rested and built the canoes for the last leg of the journey. The rivers now all flowed west to the Pacific, and Lewis and Clark led the party down the Columbia River into a land of rain forests and thick fog. On November 7, 1805, they paddled into Gray Bay,

In the Words of Lewis and Clark

President Jefferson exhorted Lewis and Clark to write down everything they saw on their expedition. The pair did not disappoint the president. Below are some excerpts of *The Lewis and Clark Expedition*, written by Meriwether Lewis and published in 1814.

On Chopunnish Indians hunting deer:

[The Indians] make use of a decoy. This consists of the skin of the head and the upper part of a neck of a deer, kept in its natural shape by a frame of small sticks on the inside. As soon as the hunter perceives a deer he conceals himself, and with his hand moves the decoy so as to represent a real deer in the act of feeding, which is done so naturally that the game is seduced within reach of arrows.

May 15, 1806

On enjoying a bath:

Our men as well as the [Willetpos] Indians amused themselves by going into the bath (a hot spring); the latter, according to their universal custom, going first into the hot bath, where they remain as long as they can bear the heat, then plunging into the creek, which is now of an icy coldness, and repeating this operation several times, but always ending with the warm bath.

June 29, 1806

On the winds of the Plains:

The winds are sometimes violent in these plains. The men inform us that as they were bringing one of the canoes along on truck-wheels, they hoisted the sail and the wind carried her along for some distance.

June 26, 1804

William Clark, depicted here as an elderly man, survived Lewis by almost 30 years.

where they could hear the roar of ocean waves pounding on the shore. "Ocean in view! Oh! The joy!" wrote Clark.

How did the Lewis and Clark journey end?

The expedition spent the winter on the coast of the Pacific, drenched by the frequent rainstorms. On March 23, 1806, they began the long trek back. One group, led by Clark, retraced the expedition's steps. Lewis led another party down the Yellowstone River, reuniting with Clark on August 12 where the Yellowstone flows into the Missouri River. The expedition sailed down the Missouri, arriving in St. Louis to a joyful welcome on September 23, 1806.

The Lewis and Clark expedition opened up the West to further exploration and, eventually, settlement. It also solved a question that had obsessed explorers for more than 300 years: No usable waterway cuts unbroken across North America.

Who was John Charles Frémont?

John Charles Frémont was born in Savannah, Georgia, in 1813. When he was 25, Frémont joined an expedition to the upper Mississippi and Missouri rivers, where he learned mapping and surveying. Missouri senator Thomas Hart Benton, who became Frémont's father-in-law in 1841, believed passionately in expanding the United States westward. To open the region to white settlers, the senator sponsored Frémont on several exploratory missions, which allowed Frémont to map much of the territory between the Mississippi River and the Pacific Ocean. On the first expedition, begun in 1842, Frémont surveyed a route through what is today Nebraska, Wyoming, and Idaho. The route would become the Oregon Trail—a highway into the West for millions of white settlers. While surveying the area, Frémont climbed what he thought was the highest peak in the Rockies (historians are uncertain which peak Frémont climbed). After returning to Washington, D.C., Frémont and his wife wrote an account of his adventures, firing the imagination of the nation to the potential of the West. In spring 1843, Frémont led a party of 40 men into the mountains again, this time to find a suitable route to the Pacific Ocean. The expedition moved west and found the Great Salt Lake in what today

Sacajawea on the $1 Coin

In 1997, Congress authorized the issuing of a new $1 gold coin with the image of Sacajawea to be inscribed on its face. The sculptor, Glenna Goodacre, used a Shoshone student as a model. Goodacre portrayed Sacajawea carrying her infant son and looking confidently back over her shoulder. With the new coin in circulation, Sacajawea has been honored along with George Washington, Thomas Jefferson, Abraham Lincoln, and others as an American hero.

The Mountainmen

As in an earlier period of North American exploration, the first white men to see this new land were usually trappers and traders. Frémont was greatly aided by the mountainmen who had already traveled in the territory—Kit Carson, Jebediah Strong Smith, Joseph Reddeford Walker, and others. These men acted as guides and provided essential information about the climate, the wildlife, and any Indian tribes they might encounter.

is Utah. Frémont turned north, reached Oregon, and then journeyed south into California. By winter 1844, the men were starving and freezing in the Sierra Nevada. The Indian guides deserted them, and Frémont and his men struggled for 30 days until finally reaching safety in Sacramento, California. In 1845, Frémont returned to the West, blazing and mapping a new trail to California. Again, Frémont wrote a stirring version of his adventures that became immensely popular with the American public, earning him the nickname "Pathfinder." Besides encouraging white settlement in the West, Frémont's expeditions made him popular enough to run for president in 1856, but he lost to James Buchanan.

Who was Alexander von Humboldt?

Alexander von Humboldt was born in Prussia in 1769 to a wealthy family. As a young boy, he explored his father's estate, keenly examining the flowering blossoms, trees, and plants. Humboldt's mother, however, disapproved of his growing interest in botany. She insisted that he study law. Humboldt obeyed and began a distinguished career in civil service. But when his mother died, Humboldt abruptly abandoned his job and about a year later, in 1799, booked passage to Mexico. "What a wealth of observation I shall collect here on the earth's construction," he wrote. "What happiness lies before me. I am dizzy with joy."

Humboldt, accompanied by a Frenchman named Aimé Bonpland, landed in Caracas, Venezuela, and began sketching and collecting samples of the flowers, trees, and

continued on page 68

Cartographer Edward Wells created this 1700 map of South America and dedicated it to the young Duke of Gloucester, an English nobleman studying geography at Oxford University. The map shows the "Country of the Amazones," the vast interior of the South Amer-ican continent, as a mysterious, unmarked area.

Alexander von Humboldt, 87 years old in this picture, appears to rest comfortably in his study, long after his arduous expeditions in South America.

continued from page 65

animals in the country. In February 1800, Humboldt and Bonpland journeyed south into the interior toward the Amazon River. The heat grew unbearable, and the party began traveling at night and dozing during the day in hammocks. The two men collected samples, even capturing electric eels in a swamp. Humboldt, impatient to understand the eels' ability to shock, placed his hands on an eel's barrel and was soon screaming in pain. The expedition continued south into jungles dense with foliage and loud with the screams of monkeys and the sinister growling of jaguars. The rivers and streams swarmed with vicious piranha, which could strip meat from bone in minutes. Humboldt was fascinated by the teeming life around him, and in his curiosity left nothing unexamined. He spent more than four years in South America and Mexico, eventually bringing 60,000 samples back to Europe. Humboldt devoted the next 23 years to sorting and publishing his findings, which eventually filled 30 volumes.

Who was Ynes Mexia?

Ynes Mexia was born in Texas in 1870, a descendant of Mexican-American settlers, and spent most of her life in Texas, Philadelphia, and Mexico City. After her husband

Ynes Mexia's passion for exploring and collecting samples of wildlife led her to Alaska, Brazil, Peru, Ecuador, Argentina, Bolivia, and Mexico.

died, she moved to San Francisco, California, and became a social worker. At the age of 51, she entered the University of California and began studying botany. Many of the plants in North and South America had not yet been identified. In 1925, she accompanied an expedition to Mexico to collect biology samples. She returned the next year to the western states of Mexico, this time traveling alone. In the following years, she collected samples in Alaska, Brazil, Peru, Ecuador, Argentina, Bolivia, and Mexico. Working mostly alone, she made cultural observations of the people she lived with and collected more than 150,000 plants, resulting in the discovery of 500 new species.

Who was Ludwig Leichhardt?

Born in Prussia in 1813, Friedrich Wilhelm Ludwig Leichhardt studied natural science and philosophy at the universities of Berlin and Göttingen. As a young man, he traveled through Europe doing fieldwork and became fluent in English, French, and Italian. In 1841, an English companion sponsored Leichhardt's voyage to Australia, where Leichhardt planned to use his skills to explore the interior of the young colony. From 1842 to 1844, Leichhardt collected plant and rock specimens in the Hunter River Valley. In 1844, he joined an overland expedition to Port Essington. But Leichhardt grew impatient with the slow pace and raised money for his own trip.

In October 1844, Leichhardt and ten men ventured into the interior of Australia, intending to blaze an overland route from Brisbane on the eastern coast to Port Essington on the northern coast. The expedition members were plagued by their inexperience. Moving only six miles a day, the expedition lost a tent and one-fifth of its flour. Two men quit. The others quarreled bitterly. Leichhardt, an ineffective leader, couldn't maintain group harmony. On June 25, 1845, one man was killed and two others wounded in an aborigine attack. By then, the tiny, weary group was on the verge of starving. Leichhardt had supplies for a seven-month journey, but food ran out. Desperate, Leichhardt used his knowledge to identify plants for food. On December 17, 1844—14 months after they began—the group reached Port Essington, where shocked townspeople greeted them as heroes. The newly world famous Leichhardt planned another journey—this time to cross the continent from east to west. In March 1848, Leichhardt led another group into the Australian wilderness on an expedition he estimated would last two years. They were never heard from again.

Who were Burke and Wills?

Explorers, such as the Englishman Matthew Flinders and the Frenchman Nicolas Baudin, had mapped most of Australia's coast by the mid-1800s. The vast interior of the continent, however, remained unexplored by Europeans. To encourage exploration, the Royal Society of Victoria sponsored an expedition to cross Australia from south to north. In August 1860, an Irishman named Robert O'Hara Burke led a party of 15 men, 28 horses, and 27 camels into the interior. The animals carried tents, guns, equipment, and stores of salted meats, lime juice, and flour—enough to feed the expedition for a year and a half. More than 10,000 people turned out in Melbourne to see the men off. Burke told them, "No expedition has ever started under such favorable circumstances as this."

But within a month, Burke had argued with his second in command and dismissed him, promoting an Englishman named William John Wills in his place. In late October, Burke realized that the increasing summer heat was drying out the landscape around him (in the Southern Hemisphere, the summer months are November, December, and January). In order to make it easier for the animals to forage, he decided to divide his party in two. Burke went ahead with Wills and six other men and their animals. The other party lagged behind, and Burke decided to continue on to the northern coast without their support. He divided his group again, this time making the final push with three other men. It took them less than two months to travel 750 miles to the sea. They passed through the sands of the Stony Desert and fields covered with spiny grass. At the beginning of February, Burke and Wills could smell the salty ocean, but swamps and showers drove them back. The men were disappointed at not seeing the ocean but thrilled to have succeeded in crossing Australia.

How did the Wills and Burke expedition end in tragedy?

The four men marked their positions and began the return to their base camp, a grueling journey that left them half-starved and one of them dead. But when they arrived, they found the camp deserted. A note explained that the supporting party had not yet brought up supplies. Concerned, the men in the camp had decided to set out south to find them. Burke, Wills, and another man named King were marooned in the middle of Australia, hundreds of miles from help, with only a box containing 40 days' worth of food left there by the other party. Weak and desperate, the men tried to reach a sheep station called Mount Hopeless to the southwest. After 60 days, the three men had eaten all their food and had slaughtered their camels. Wills and Burke both died around June 28. Found and kept alive by aborigines, King survived to recount what happened. The bodies of Burke and Wills were recovered and they were buried as heroes in Melbourne.

Who was Mungo Park?

Mungo Park was the seventh of 12 children born to a family in Scotland. He studied medicine and accompanied an expedition to Africa as the surgeon in 1792. In 1795, the African Association appointed Park to look for a giant waterway that supposedly ran westward through Africa and emptied out of the western coast into the Atlantic Ocean. In December 1795, Park left Bathurst, a city on Africa's west coast, with two servants and traveled into the interior, through parts of present-day Gambia, Guinea, and Mali. Almost immediately, Park was forced to pay tribute to the local king—which cost him most of his tobacco. In the Medina kingdom, Park was greeted warmly by King Jatta. Jatta warned him of the dangers ahead, but Park was persistent, and Jatta agreed to furnish him with a guide. Park continued on. Some kings robbed him of his possessions and supplies. Park was able to impress others with his surgical skills.

In February 1796, Park crossed into Ludamar, where he was imprisoned by the Islamic ruler. The king accused Park and his companions of being spies. He threatened to cut off their hands and poke out their eyes. After five months in captivity, Park stole a horse and escaped. Without food or water, Park struggled on alone. Exhausted and starving, he stumbled into a Fulani village, where a woman fed him and his horse. Park joined two African travelers, who led him to his goal—the Niger River. Park was the first European to see this great river and describe its eastward flow. On July 30, he began the long trek back to the coast, finally arriving in mid-June 1797.

After returning to Scotland, Park planned to settle down as a country doctor. But in 1803, the African Association asked him to return and chart the Niger River. Park's medical practice was not doing as well as he had hoped, so he agreed. In May 1804, Park led 45 men on the same path he had used earlier. But he soon faced disaster. The rainy season began, soaking the men and bogging them down in mud. The local kings demanded tribute. After three months, 33 men and all the animals were dead. The survivors continued on in a rigged boat but were mistaken for slave traders. They were attacked, and Park is believed to have drowned.

Who was Heinrich Barth?

Heinrich Barth, born in 1821 in Germany, was a very serious student. When he went to the University of Berlin, he studied so hard that his father feared he had no friends. Hoping to cure his son of his shyness, his father sent him on a tour of Paris, London, and the North African coast. The trip did little for Barth's social ability, but he was fascinated by Africa. At age 28, he joined an English expedition led by a former missionary, James Richardson. In March 1850, the party left the Libyan city of Tripoli and journeyed into the Sahara Desert. About 500 miles south of Tripoli, Barth discovered rock paintings thousands of years old. They depicted the Sahara as it changed from fertile plains into a vast desert.

After a year of travel, Richardson died of malaria, and Barth took over the expedition. Though usually shy and awkward, Barth proved adept at impressing the sultans of the kingdoms through which he traveled. He showered them with expensive gifts, and they received him warmly.

The Royal Geographical Society

In 1830, a group of Englishmen founded the Royal Geographical Society in London as an organization to advance geographic knowledge. The society promoted and supported many of the expeditions into Africa in the 1800s and Antarctica in the early 1900s. Today, the society has a membership of about 13,000.

While a companion explored Lake Chad—a lake in west central Africa—Barth discovered parts of the Benue River and the Shari River. He planned to travel to Timbuktu along roads made dangerous by robbers. To fool them, Barth pretended to be delivering religious books to the leader of Timbuktu. The ruse worked, and Barth and his men entered the city safely. For two more years, Barth explored West Africa, finally returning to Tripoli in August 1855. He soon returned to Europe, having spent nearly six years in Africa. Barth devoted the next three years to recording his experiences in a book. Many contemporary readers found his writing tedious. Later, Barth's attention to detail and keen eye for observation would earn him praise as one of Africa's greatest explorers.

What was one of the greatest mysteries for European explorers of Africa?

In the 1860s, a husband and wife team attempted to solve one of the most elusive geographical mysteries—the source of the Nile, the world's longest river at 4,132 miles. The waterway flowed north through Egypt, nourishing crops and providing the base for the Egyptian empire. Explorers both ancient and modern had speculated on and sought its source for thousands of years. On December 18, 1862, an Englishman named Samuel Baker and his wife, Florence, embarked on a journey to solve the mystery. Beginning at the city of Khartoum, Sudan, they led an expedition of about 100 men, four horses, four camels, and 21 donkeys in three boats. But after just two months of travel, the party met two half-starved English explorers named John Hanning Speke and James Grant, who had also been seeking the source of the Nile. Speke explained that he had returned to Lake Victoria, which he had found and named in 1858. (Lake Victoria, second-largest freshwater lake in the world, extends into present-day Tanzania, Uganda, and Kenya.) This time, Speke was certain that the lake was the source of the Nile. Bitterly disappointed, Baker asked if there was anything left to discover. Speke replied that he had not been able to follow the river from Lake Victoria as it flowed downstream. A large part of the Nile remained unexplored. Inspired again, the Bakers bid farewell to Speke and Grant and continued southward overland.

What did the Bakers find?

The Bakers spent the next nine months crossing through the African wilderness or waiting in villages because civil wars made travel too dangerous. The Bakers were a formidable pair. Samuel was hot tempered and decisive. Florence was quick witted, well organized, and patient. Together, they endured travel through mountainous terrain that killed most of their animals. In January

Samuel and Florence Baker made one of the most famous husband-wife exploratory teams in history. Their complementary personalities proved to be a great asset in their adventures.

1864, they entered an area in present-day Uganda ruled by a king named Kamrasi. Needing Kamrasi's permission to continue south, Samuel began swapping gifts with the king. Eventually, Samuel had little left to give. Kamrasi asked for his guns and navigation tools. Samuel refused. Kamrasi made a final request—Florence. Samuel pulled a revolver from his holster and pointed it at the king while Florence gave a fiery speech in Arabic. The king was shocked; he thought Samuel would be pleased to swap wives. The Bakers left Kamrasi two days later. On March 14, the party at last glimpsed the silver sheen of a massive lake. Here, the Bakers were convinced, lay the true source of the Nile River (later, this was proved wrong). Samuel named it Lake Albert, after the English prince. The return trip down the Nile took another 18 months. After the Bakers returned to England, Samuel was knighted and the Royal Geographical Society awarded him the Victoria Gold Medal, its most coveted award.

Who was David Livingstone?

David Livingstone was born in Scotland in 1813. After studying medicine, Livingstone went to Africa as a missionary in 1841. By 1843, Livingstone had ventured into Kuruman, an isolated area in present-day South Africa, where he founded a missionary station in the village of Mabotsa. There, while Livingstone tried to convert natives to Christianity, a lion pounced on him, mauling his left arm before being frightened away by gunshots. Livingstone would never be able to lift the arm above his shoulder again.

Livingstone grew discouraged, feeling that the Africans did not take Christianity seriously, and he believed that the tribal culture would have to be destroyed before they accepted Christianity. To do that, theorized Livingstone, Africa needed more trade with Europe. Seeking to find a navigable waterway across the continent, Livingstone traveled north from Mabotsa in 1849. After covering 700 miles, he discovered a broad waterway that flowed east called the Zambezi River. Here, exclaimed Livingstone, is the highway for British commerce and Christianity to penetrate Africa. In 1853, Livingstone turned west and plunged into Angola. Perhaps he sought a connection between the

African Explorers of Africa

Before the 1800s, Africa was seen by Europeans mainly as a source of gold, ivory, and slaves. Europe in the mid-1800s was in the midst of an industrial boom. Flush with power and confidence, the Europeans looked to Africa as a source for raw materials for their industries and a place to spread Christianity. Knowing very little about the interior of the continent, white European explorers plunged into the land they called the "dark continent."

But, as an African statesman later said, "there was nothing to discover, we were here all the time." European claims of being the first to complete a journey were often exaggerated or wrong. Muslim traders had traveled through most of Africa, and many European explorers accompanied slave caravans. The English explorer David Livingstone claimed in 1856 to be the first person to cross the continent. But the feat had been performed 50 years earlier by two Arab-Portuguese slave traders, Pedro Baptista and Anastasio José. Most European explorers did not acknowledge their achievement.

Zambezi River and the Atlantic Ocean. Traveling through this terrain, with its lush jungles, fields covered in sharp grass, and swamps swarming with mosquitoes, left Livingstone feverish and weak. After six months, he arrived on the coast of the Atlantic Ocean. Despite his exhaustion, he wrote of his journeys, prepared meticulous maps, and sent them to England, where his exploits were applauded. But by that time, Livingstone was crossing east again, growing partially deaf in one ear from rheumatic fever and almost losing an eye to a sharp branch. On November 17, 1855, Livingstone stumbled upon a 300-foot-high waterfall more than a mile wide, thundering in clouds of mists. He named it Victoria Falls after Queen Victoria of Great Britain. (The falls are on the Zambezi River, which borders present-day Zambia and Zimbabwe.) When Livingstone returned to England in 1856, he was showered with medals and praise for his discoveries.

How was Livingstone rescued?

The 43-year-old explorer returned to Africa in 1858 and led a disastrous expedition up the Zambezi River. The

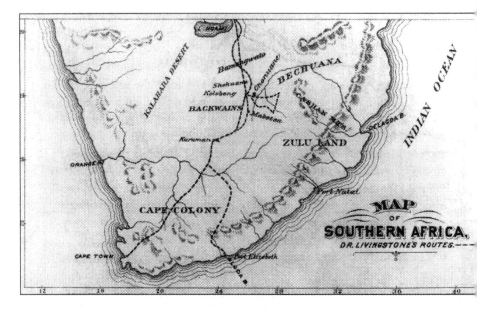

MAP of SOUTHERN AFRICA.
DR. LIVINGSTONE'S ROUTES.---

This map shows the routes that David Livingstone took on his first journey into South Africa, in 1849.

river was blocked by foaming rapids, Livingstone's miserable European companions quarreled, and three of them were killed in local tribal wars. In 1866, Livingstone led another exploring party into eastern Africa hoping to find the source of the Nile River. By 1868, Livingstone had entered Lake Bangweulu (in present-day Zambia), an area of leech-infested swamps. Weakened by fever, Livingstone joined an Arab slave caravan and continued seeking his elusive quarry through 1870. By this time, people began to wonder what had happened to him, as news from Livingstone had not reached the outside world for years. The *New York Herald* newspaper sent a journalist, a British-American named Henry Morton Stanley, to find the explorer.

In November 1871, Livingstone was lying exhausted in Ujiji, a village on the bank of Lake Tanganyika, a lake that today forms the border between Congo and Tanzania. On November 10, he heard a commotion and saw a crowd with an American flag marching down the street. Livingstone rose and to his shock saw a white man dressed in flannel clothing and freshly waxed boots. Stanley saw Livingstone and uttered his now famous line, "Dr. Livingstone I presume?" Livingstone had been found. Livingstone died in May 1873. His black porters, who had journeyed with him faithfully for so many years, carried his body 1,000 miles, a trek that lasted almost a year, to the coast, where it was transported back to England for burial.

Who was Henry Morton Stanley?

In 1874, Stanley resolved to explore more of Africa and determine once and for all the source of the Nile River. Using his reputation as the savior of Livingstone, he gathered sponsors to finance an exploring party that arrived on the shores of Lake Victoria in February 1875. After exploring the coasts of the lake, he ventured south and then west, where he discovered a river, nearly a mile wide, flowing north. In November 1876, Stanley led 356 men into the jungles bordering the river—land that had never been seen by Europeans. When the men put a boat onto the river, they heard calls relayed through the forest. Africans were warning one another of strangers in a boat. "Reed arrows, tipped with poison, were shot at us from the jungles as we glided by," recalled Stanley. "Out of every bush glared eyes flaming with hate; in the stream lurked the crocodiles to feed."

Sidi Mubarak Bombay

Sidi Mubarak Bombay, who was born about 1820 in east Africa, played an important role in most of the European exploration of Africa during the 1850s, 1860s, and 1870s. Bombay first served as a soldier with the English explorers Sir Richard Burton and John Hanning Speke on their expedition to find the source of the Nile in 1857. In 1860, Speke hired Bombay again, who arranged the supplies and hired the porters to carry them. In 1871, Henry Morton Stanley arrived in Africa to search for David Livingstone. Needing help to provision the expedition, Stanley turned to Bombay, who by then had a reputation as an efficient organizer and an effective leader of porters and soldiers. In 1874, Verney Lovett Cameron sought out Bombay when he organized a caravan to explore Lake Tanganyika in south central Africa. While Cameron lay ill, Bombay explored most of the lake. In recognition of Bombay's contributions to European exploration, he was awarded a life pension by the Royal Geographical Society in 1876. Bombay, who was already engaged on another expedition when he heard the news, promptly quit and retired. He died in 1885.

For weeks, the party continued down the river in their canoes. At one spot, Stanley and his party, now down to a little more than 100 men, faced 54 canoes filled with African warriors, possibly more than 2,000 in all. Stanley's men battled desperately and used their guns to a decisive advantage. After 32 skirmishes, Stanley and the men entered a safe territory along the river where they were welcomed enthusiastically by a chief. Stanley asked the chief the name of the river. "Ikutu Ya Kongo," he answered. Stanley named the river Congo. As the party continued downriver, the water grew treacherous. The canoes entered the foaming maelstrom of the river's rapids, where whirlpools swamped one canoe and crushed another against rocks. In one afternoon, nine men were drowned, a tragedy so devastating to Stanley that he considered suicide. The river was too dangerous, and Stanley ordered his men to abandon the crafts and continue on foot. In August 1876, Stanley and 108 men arrived at the mouth of the river where it emptied into the Atlantic Ocean. The river system of the Congo was opened to Europeans. Back in England, Stanley wrote *Through the Dark Continent*, an immensely popular account of his journey.

Who was Mary Kingsley?

Dressed in a prim, dark dress, Mary Kingsley appeared to be a proper Englishwoman of the Victorian Era. But she was also one of its greatest and bravest explorers. Born in 1862, Kingsley spent her youth in seclusion, rarely leaving her home. When she was 29, both her mother and father died within months of each other, and her brother left to travel east. Devastated, she took a holiday in the Canary Islands, where she heard colorful stories about Africa from sea captains and traders. Her imagination ignited, she visited the ports of West Africa in 1893, delighting in the exotic markets and people.

In December 1894, Kingsley returned to Africa, this time determined to explore parts of the continent and send samples of fish and beetles back to the British Museum for study. Kingsley did not act like most previous European visitors. While the male explorers relied on guns and surrounded themselves with armed escorts, Kingsley used her self-confidence and a shrewd ability to trade. On July 22, 1895, Kingsley entered the territory of Gabon in the French Congo and traveled up the Ogooué River. Kingsley knew the region was inhabited by the Fang, a tribe rumored to be cannibals, but she forged ahead, paddling with guides and stopping at villages to trade. After seven days and 70 miles, her voyage ended. She had safely negotiated with tribes that routinely killed and ate prisoners. When she returned to England she published an account, *Travels in West Africa*. The book was an immediate success, but her harsh condemnation of European exploitation in Africa brought severe criticism. "What we do in Africa today," she wrote, "a thousand years hence there will be Africans to thrive or suffer for it."

Who was Isabella Bird Bishop?

Isabella Bird Bishop, an Englishwoman born in 1831, lost both her parents by the time she was 24. Afterward, she suffered from depression, backaches, and insomnia. When her doctor recommended a change of scenery, Bishop set sail for Australia in July 1872. Six months later, she took another ship across the South Pacific to the Hawaiian Islands. A hurricane threatened to send the ship to the bot-

Isabella Bird Bishop spent much of her travels in the shelter of tents. Her great endurance and tolerance of rough conditions allowed her to travel for months at a time.

tom, but Bishop was thrilled by the adventure. In Hawaii, she watched women as well as men straddle horses while riding. (In Europe, a woman was expected to ride "sidesaddle," with both legs on one side.) Bishop broke tradition, rode "cavalier fashion," and loved it. Bishop found the power and beauty of nature irresistible. She scrambled to the tops of volcanoes to watch them erupt into streams of lava. A torrent of water flowing through a gulch almost drowned her when she attempted to cross it. Drenched, exhausted, bruised—she had never felt better.

Bishop left Hawaii, sailed to the United States, and journeyed into the rugged peaks of the Rocky Mountains. She worked alongside cowboys and drove cattle. One of her guides, Rocky Mountain Jim, was so smitten that he asked her to marry him. But she refused him. "He is a man any woman might love," she wrote, "but no sane woman would marry." Bishop traveled on to Japan, China, and Indochina (now Vietnam) before returning to England and marrying an Englishman. She wrote books of her travels that became enormously popular.

At the age of 58, Bishop traveled with missionaries to India, Turkey, and Persia. At age 70, she rode by camel 1,000 miles across Morocco. She wrote of her experiences and described the people, but she was always drawn most to the awesome spectacle of nature. And she never wearied of her travels. Despite frail health, Bishop could eat anything and sleep anywhere. "She has the appetite of a tiger and the digestion of an ostrich," wrote her husband. Bishop seemed to thrive on discomfort. When she died at age 79 in England, her trunks were packed for a trip to China.

Who was Lawrence of Arabia?

Thomas Edward Lawrence, born in 1888, grew up in Oxford, England, where he attended the High School and Jesus College. As a student, he was fascinated by medieval military architecture and in 1909 he visited France. He pedaled his bicycle through the French countryside and stopped to sketch castles. He then went to Syria and Palestine (modern-day Israel) and compared the French castles to those left behind by the Christian crusaders. His thesis on the subject won him great acclaim, but his exposure to the Middle East would change his life. While traveling to Syria, he was attacked by a mob and beaten. An Arab family took in the injured Lawrence and nursed him back to health. Lawrence grew to admire the Arabs. In 1911, he joined an archaeological expedition in the Mesopotamian region. World War I broke out in 1914, pitting Germany, Austria, and Turkey against England, France, and Russia. Lawrence returned to the Middle East and helped map the Sinai peninsula for the British. In late 1914, Lawrence was made an intelligence officer in the Middle East and he urged that the British support Arab revolts in Arabia against the Turkish empire. Lawrence joined the Arab guerrilla operations and organized them to attack the Turkish army. His exploits became legend and newspaper reporters referred to him as "Lawrence of Arabia." Lawrence recounted his adventures in a book, *The Seven Pillars of Wisdom*, published in 1927.

Who was Gertrude Bell?

Gertrude Bell, born in 1868 in Durham, England, attended Lady Margaret Hall at Oxford, where she graduated with high honors in history. Bell first traveled to the Middle East in 1892—"the place I have always longed to see," she wrote to a friend. She visited her uncle, who was the British ambassador to Tehran, a city in Persia (modern-day Iran). Quickly learning Persian, Bell translated Persian poetry into English. In 1899, she went to Jerusalem to study Arabic and visited Lebanon and Jordan to see ancient Roman ruins. Bell began to travel extensively, going around the world twice before returning to the Middle East in 1905. This time, she traveled through Syria into Turkey, living in tents and staying in houses with friends of her family. Except for her Arab servants, Bell went alone, and she was often the first European woman to see the sights of the Middle East. She wrote about her experiences in *Syria: Desert and the Sown* (1907). In 1909, Bell traveled down the Euphrates River to Baghdad. In 1913, she visited Ha'il, a city in the center of Arabia rarely visited by Westerners. During World War I (1914–1918), Bell used her extensive knowledge of the Middle East to help the English encourage revolt among the Arabs. In 1917, Bell set-

continued on page 86

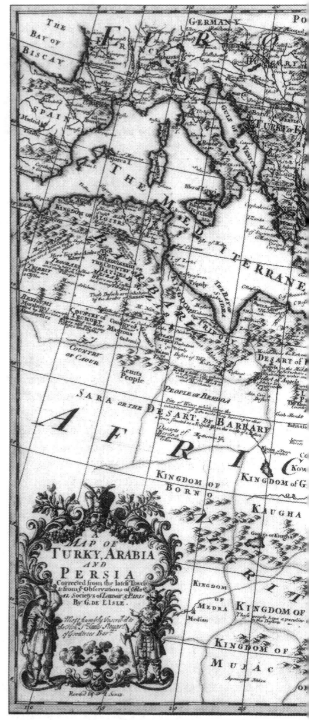

This 1721 map reveals that the geography of the Middle East was well known to Europeans, but the cultures there remained for the most part unfamiliar. Nineteenth-century explorers such as Isabella Bird Bishop and Gertrude Bell regarded the area as mysterious, and avid readers of their books considered the tales of their travels to be quite exciting and exotic.

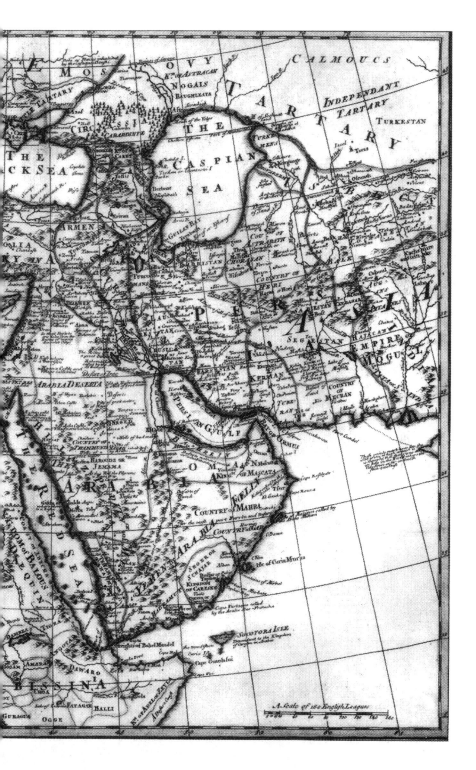

Shown here dressed in traveling clothing, Nellie Bly became world famous when she traveled around the world in 72 days, 6 hours, 11 minutes, and 14 seconds.

continued from page 83

tled in Baghdad, which became her home for the rest of her life.

Who was Nellie Bly?

In 1885, Elizabeth Cochrane read an article titled "What Good Are Girls For?" in the *Pittsburgh Gazette*. The article concluded that they weren't worth much. Cochrane, infuriated, fired off an angry letter to the editor. The editor was impressed by Cochrane's spirit and her writing ability. Far from being offended, he offered her a job. At the *Gazette*, Cochrane began using a pen name that would one day be world famous—Nellie Bly. Cochrane first wrote about Pittsburgh's poor and then traveled to Mexico, where she described the corruption of the government. Angered by her harsh criticism, the Mexicans expelled her. Cochrane left Pittsburgh to work for Joseph Pulitzer's *New York World*. For one story, she pretended to be insane in order to be committed to an asylum for ten days. Her writings on the horrible treatment of the insane led to outrage and reform. On November 14, 1889, Cochrane began her greatest adventure. The Frenchman Jules Verne had written a novel called *Around the World in 80 Days*. Cochrane decided to go around the world in a shorter amount of time. Traveling on ships, trains, wagons, rickshas, and sampans, Cochrane circled the globe, returning to New York City 72 days, 6 hours, 11 minutes, and 14 seconds after her departure. She later wrote *Around the World in Seventy-two Days*, an immensely popular book that won her acclaim.

Who was Alexandra David-Neel?

No European had ever been permitted to enter the city of Lhasa, Tibet, the home of the sacred Dalai Lama, the Buddhist leader of Tibet. In 1924, however, a 55-year-old Frenchwoman, her skin dyed and hair dark with ink, dressed like a Mongolian peasant, entered the forbidden city. Accompanied only by her adopted son, she traveled at night and rested during the day. Once, the pair was ambushed by robbers; the woman fired her pistol and scared them off. Finally, she entered Lhasa and then returned to tell the world of its marvels. Her name, Alexandra David-Neel, became famous around the world.

David-Neel was born into a wealthy family in France in 1868. As a teenaged girl, she showed an independent spirit and a disregard for what others thought of her. She traveled alone by bike to Spain and by train to Italy, actions thought scandalous at the time. When she turned 21, she became fascinated with eastern religions and spent her family inher-

Alexandra David-Neel became the first European to successfully visit Lhasa, Tibet, the home of the sacred Dalai Lama.

itance to visit India and Sri Lanka. She returned to Europe in 1893, studied music, and traveled through eastern Asia, North Africa, and the Mediterranean, performing on the piano and singing. But she could not shake her fascination with the East. She wrote a book on Buddhism and in 1912 traveled to the northeastern Indian border. There, she met the Dalai Lama, who had fled his country because of a Chinese invasion. She lived in a mountain cave for several months, entered a Buddhist monastery, and met a 15-year-old boy, Aphur Yongden, whom she later adopted. In October 1917, David-Neel traveled westward from Beijing through China, a 2,000-mile journey through countryside torn by war. Eventually reaching Kumbum, a city on the border of China and Tibet, in 1920 she stayed three years and translated Buddhist texts into French. In 1923, she began her famous journey into Lhasa and in 1924 became the first European to lay eyes on the sacred city.

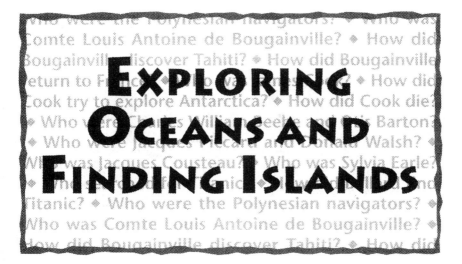

EXPLORING OCEANS AND FINDING ISLANDS

Who were the Polynesian navigators?

The Polynesians had traveled from Asia into the hundreds of islands of the South Pacific centuries before the Europeans sailed the Pacific Ocean. The Polynesians navigated the ocean in giant canoes, some up to 100 feet long. To construct a more seaworthy ship, they laid two canoes side by side and secured a deck across the middle. The decks of these sturdy craft provided a platform on which to fish, cook, and carry goods and passengers. A sail was hung on a mast to harness the wind. Using the stars as a guide, the Polynesians sailed among the hundreds of islands of the South Pacific, waging war, trading, and settling new territories. In the 1700s, the English explorer James Cook was astounded by the extent of the Polynesian settlements.

Who was Comte Louis Antoine de Bougainville?

In 1763, the French signed a treaty with the English that ended the French and Indian Wars. The treaty marked a shattering defeat for the French, as it gave the English all of the formerly French colonies in North America. With the Northern Hemisphere closed to the French, a French soldier named Louis Antoine de Bougainville led a 400-man crew into the vast, uncharted waters of the Pacific Ocean. The French king Louis XV hoped Bougainville would discover new lands brimming with spices and jewels to add to the French Empire. Bougainville left France on November 15,

Thor Heyerdahl

Scientists and historians have long debated whether ancient cultures crossed the world's oceans thousands of years before Columbus. One Norwegian, named Thor Heyerdahl, decided to test the theory with action. While living on Fatu Hiva island in the South Pacific, Heyerdahl listened as the people told him they had originally come from lands to the east—South America. Later, Heyerdahl found similarities between stone carvings on Fatu Hiva and the wooden poles fashioned by Indians in the Pacific Northwest. He theorized that American Indians had migrated from South America to the South Pacific islands. Not content to theorize, in 1947 Heyerdahl built a 45-foot raft of logs and bamboo and set himself and five crewmen adrift from Peru. The ocean currents pulled the raft north and then west into the open ocean. After drifting for 101 days and 4,300 miles, Heyerdahl and his men reached the Tuamotu Islands in the South Pacific. Bolstered by this success, Heyerdahl next wondered about the similarity between Egyptian pyramids and the pyramids of central America. In 1969, he constructed a papyrus-reed boat and voyaged across the Atlantic from North Africa to Barbados, an island off North America. Heyerdahl's theories were extremely controversial, and historians and anthropologists still argue whether his voyages are proof of early sea travel. Yet his journeys represent contemporary examples of the daring of early explorers.

1766, in a sturdy 26-gun frigate called *La Boudeuse*, with a supply ship following close behind. Storms forced repairs, and it took more than a year for Bougainville to sail south and navigate through the treacherous Strait of Magellan. On January 26, 1768, the two ships entered the Pacific, sending a surge of joy through captain and crew. For the next three months, *La Boudeuse* sailed steadily across the South Pacific. Bougainville took precautions to sterilize the water and keep his crew healthy, but without fruit and vegetables, some grew ill with scurvy. Finally, on March 22, an island surrounded by beach with patches of forest appeared on the horizon. An excited Bougainville ordered the ship closer. They were blocked by a reef of razor-sharp coral that surrounded the island like a wall. Disappointed, *La Boudeuse* and the supply ship had to sail on.

How did Bougainville discover Tahiti?

Eleven days later, on April 2, 1768, the sailors on *La Boudeuse* spotted a dark green island rising out of the Pacific. It took Bougainville and his crew four days to navigate through the reefs surrounding the island. Swarms of islanders canoed out from the island and surrounded the ship in an excited welcome. Bougainville noted that many of the canoes were filled with beautiful women, and that it was hard "to keep 400 young French sailors, who had seen no women for six months," at their posts. The island, called Tahiti, seemed to Bougainville like a tropical paradise filled with happy people living in innocence. The Frenchmen stayed on the island for nine days, enjoying the scenery and hospitality, but also noticing that the Tahitians were expert pickpockets and stole things with glee. Bougainville, his food stores dwindling, wanted to continue west. He claimed the island for France and continued on.

How did Bougainville return to France?

La Boudeuse stopped at several other islands, but very few of them were as beautiful and hospitable as Tahiti. On one island, the natives suffered from disease and attacked the Frenchmen when they attempted to trade for food. Bougainville named it the Isle of Lepers. By the end of May, supplies were seriously low, and Bougainville and his crew were forced to kill and eat rats. In June, the ship

continued on page 94

Baré: The First Woman to Circumnavigate the World

While Bougainville's expedition sailed in the South Pacific, a rumor spread through the two ships that Bougainville eventually had to investigate. A servant appeared smooth skinned, had a feminine shape, and took strict precautions not to be seen while changing clothing. "When I came on board," wrote Bougainville, "Baré, with her face bathed in tears, owned to me that she was a woman . . . that well she knew when she embarked that we were going around the world, and that such a voyage had raised her curiosity." By disguising herself as a man, Baré became the first woman to circumnavigate the world.

Cook's voyages throughout the Pacific
Ocean added vastly to Europeans'
geographic knowledge. This map,
created in the mid-1700s, shows details
of his routes and explorations.

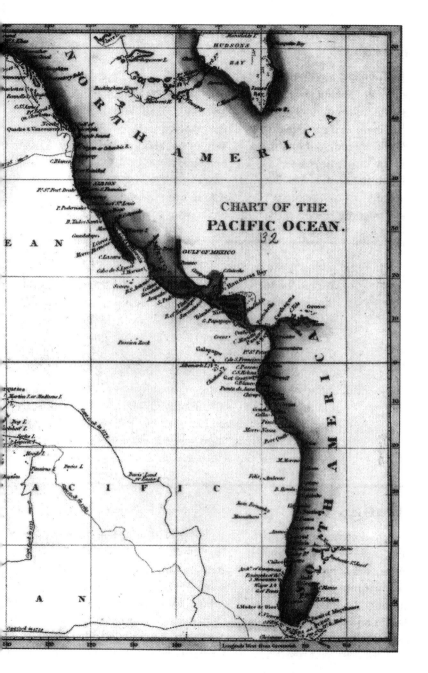

Ahutora

As the French were leaving Tahiti, the Tahitian chief begged Bougainville to take Ahutora, a young Tahitian, as a parting gift. Bougainville agreed, and Ahutora endured the next two years of voyage with the French, arriving safely in Paris in 1769. Ahutora became a celebrity among the French, who considered him a pure and noble savage. Though Ahutora adapted to French culture, developed a taste for French wine and music, and had love affairs, he grew homesick. With Bougainville's help, Ahutora boarded a ship headed to Tahiti, but he died of smallpox along the way.

continued from page 91

approached the Great Barrier Reef off the coast of Australia. Bougainville, however, directed his ship north to avoid the treacherous coral and did not discover the giant continent behind it. By late June, the sailors had grown so hungry that Bougainville was forced to issue orders forbidding them to eat leather. Battered by storms and rain, the ships maneuvered among dangerous currents, coral reefs, and islands. Food was difficult to find. Many of the islands had already been explored by other Europeans, and the natives attacked the white men when they appeared and forced them to flee. On another island, the sailors discovered

Australia

In the second century, Greek astronomer Claudius Ptolemy proposed an incorrect but influential theory. He knew of Europe and the civilizations surrounding the Mediterranean Sea. He also knew of the Middle East and had a dim knowledge of the massive Asian continent beyond it. But, he wondered, how could the earth spin and not wobble off balance, when all the land seemed to be in the Northern Hemisphere? He theorized that a giant continent must exist in the Southern Hemisphere to balance the lands of the north. He called this imaginary place *Terra Australis Incognita*, meaning "unknown southern land." Centuries later, European explorers, such as James Cook and Comte Louis Antoine de Bougainville, sailed in search of this land.

fresh water, but were unable to fish because of sea snakes and scorpions. In August, the last of the ship's food was gone, and the crew despaired when the first sailor died of scurvy. "People have long argued about the location of hell," wrote Bougainville. "Frankly, we have discovered it." Finally, on August 30, the weary crew spotted a Dutch settlement on Buru Island. The half-starved crew was treated to a sumptuous meal by their Dutch hosts. After resting and refitting, Bougainville set sail and arrived in France seven and a half months later to a hero's welcome.

Who was James Cook?

James Cook was born in Marton, Yorkshire. When he was a teenager, Cook worked in a store in a coastal town, which introduced him to the ocean and ships. At 18, Cook was apprenticed to a shipowner and learned to sail and navigate in the North Sea. After several years, Cook, longing for more adventure and advancement, joined the Royal Navy. His ability to command won him notice, and he rose in rank. In 1768, he took a party of scientists aboard H.M.S. *Endeavour* and sailed to Tahiti, where they recorded an astronomical event called the Transit of Venus. When the observation was finished, Cook opened a secret packet of instructions from the British Navy that ordered him to sail south to chart and explore the great southern continent. In July 1769, Cook ordered the *Endeavour* to weigh anchor and set sail due south. He passed through a knot of islands and continued on, the weather growing chillier. By early September, the lookouts had seen nothing but the gray swells of the sea. Convinced that no land existed farther south, Cook turned west. After another month, the crew spotted the forested hills of New Zealand. Cook used his superb mapmaking skills to chart the coast of the island. The *Endeavour* then resumed its western course and hit the Great Barrier Reef along Australia's northeastern coast. Cook knew of the existence of the continent, but its coastline had not been mapped. Cook sailed carefully along the reef, still considered one of the most dangerous areas for a ship in the world.

On June 11, the *Endeavour* lurched, and the crew heard the horrifying sound of coral punching through the

James Cook, the determined English explorer and map-maker, explored the islands of the Pacific Ocean in four extensive voyages.

ship's wooden hull. The ship shuddered to a stop, stuck fast to the reef. The crew frantically dumped more than 50 tons of stores to lighten the ship. The tide rose, and the crew pulled desperately on the anchor and finally freed the ship, though seawater flooded into the hull faster than the pumps could remove it. Cook navigated the crippled ship into a river mouth, where carpenters spent the next seven weeks patching the hull. The *Endeavour* returned to sea, and Cook led the ship home, arriving in July 1771.

How did Cook try to explore Antarctica?

Within a year of returning from his first voyage, Cook led another expedition into the South Pacific, this time on a vessel called the *Resolution*. Again, Cook plunged into the chilly waters of the southern oceans. In December, Cook wrote, "We were stopped by an immense field of ice, to which we could see no end." Tentatively, Cook moved along the ice, sailing farther south than any other explorer. Still, sheets of ice stretched to the horizon, and Cook glimpsed no mountains, no land, and no evidence of a southern continent. He turned north to the tropical waters of the South Pacific, gathering information and charting the hundreds of islands that dot the vast ocean. Still seeking to explore, he returned to the frigid waters in the south and sailed around Antarctica in a vast circle. Ice choked the rigging and Cook ordered the ship's tailor to make warmer, thicker clothes for the crew. "The cold, so intense as hardly to be endured," wrote Cook, "the whole Sea in a manner covered with ice, a hard gale and thick fog." Again, Cook was stopped by a wall of ice. In July 1775, Cook arrived safely back in England after sailing 70,000 miles. Proclaimed a hero, Cook was awarded a pension and a promotion.

How did Cook die?

Incredibly, Cook soon grew restless. In July 1776, Cook led two ships, the *Resolution* and the *Discovery*, back into the unknown. This time, Cook hoped to find the Holy Grail of explorers—the Northwest Passage through North America. Cook sailed through the Indian Ocean, around Australia, and in among the islands that were by now familiar to him. On January 18, 1778, Cook spotted a string of magnificent islands, rising like green jewels out of the Pacific Ocean. He named them the Sandwich Islands. Today, they are called Hawaii. Cook continued east, sighting the Oregon coast on March 7. He turned north and sailed along the North American coast until he entered the Bering Strait, which separates Asia and North America. No passage broke the coastline. As it had been around Antarctica, Cook's ship was wrapped in bitter cold. The men shot giant walruses for food. Cook continued into the Arctic and was halted by a wall of ice 12 feet thick.

continued on page 100

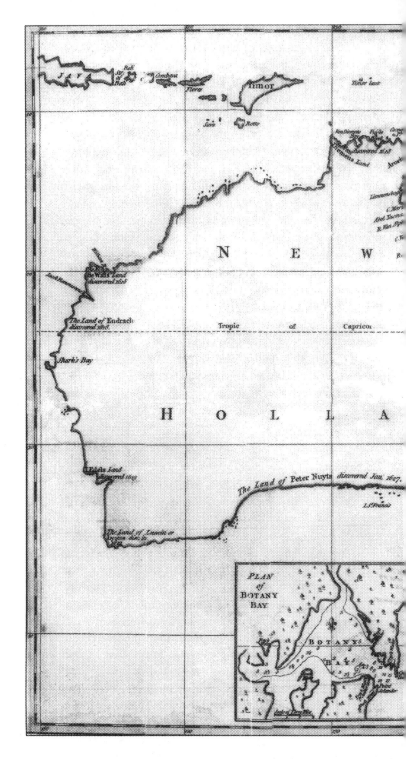

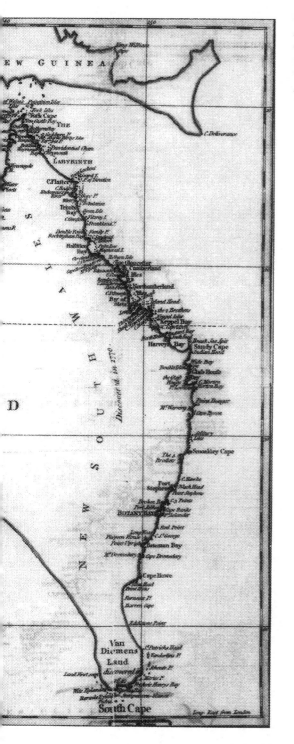

Europeans' early knowledge of Australia was limited to its eastern coast, as this eighteenth-century map reveals. The interior, thoroughly traveled by generations of Australian Aborigines, remained unexplored by colonists well into the 1800s.

continued from page 97

Disappointed but vowing to return, Cook turned back south and arrived in Hawaii on January 17, 1779. This time, Cook encountered a group of Hawaiians who considered him a returning god. They piled gifts of food at his feet and Cook could do nothing to halt their generosity. But when he realized that the natives were depriving themselves of food for his sake, Cook hastily gave the order to sail. Unfortunately, the next day a storm split the sails and snapped the mast, forcing Cook to return. The natives, who had been angered and betrayed by Cook's sudden departure, received him coldly and began to steal items from the ships. When a large boat disappeared from the *Discovery*, Cook stormed ashore with a party of armed men and tried to take the king of Hawaii hostage. A battle took place on the beach, and Cook was stabbed fatally in the back. Saddened but determined to carry on Cook's mission, his captains returned to the Bering Strait. They were blocked again by ice, forcing them to return to England by sailing back across the Pacific and around the tip of Africa. Thousands in England mourned Cook's death. The skeleton of Cook's body was recovered and buried at sea on February 21, 1779. He was posthumously awarded a coat of arms with the inscription: "He left nothing unattempted."

Who were Charles William Beebe and Otis Barton?

Covering three-quarters of Earth's surface, the ocean is the last frontier of exploration on our planet. Water pressure could overwhelm a diver below 200 feet and submarines before 1930 could dive no lower than 600 feet. The average depth of the ocean is 12,450 feet. In 1928, an engineer named Otis Barton presented a plan for a deep-sea craft to Charles William Beebe, who was director of the Department of Tropical Research at the New York Zoological Society. Barton planned to descend into the dark depths in a sturdy metal sphere just four feet in diameter. He called it a bathysphere, after two Greek words meaning "deep" and "ball." Beebe liked the simplicity of the design and two years later he joined Barton off Bermuda for the first in a series of dives.

Held by a strand of steel cable from a floating ship and supplied with oxygen tanks, the craft carried the men into the depths, farther than any living person had yet gone. There, through two windows made of quartz, Beebe reported seeing "a world as strange as Mars or Venus." Fish that had only been seen in fishermen's nets swam past their windows. On the first expedition, Beebe and Barton descended to 1,426 feet, a world record. In 1932, they went deeper, to 2,220 feet. In hushed tones, Beebe described the brilliant sea animals on a live radio broadcast. As the craft descended farther, he ran out of words. Many of the fish had never been seen before. One fish, which Beebe called the dragonfish, grew to six feet and carried a jaw full of sharp teeth. Another, called an avocet eel, was slender like a snake and displayed brilliant patterns of light. Beebe later described them as "one of the loveliest things I have ever seen." On August 14, 1934, Beebe and Barton took their last, and deepest dive, together, ending at 3,028 feet. The record would hold for fifteen years.

Who were Jacques Piccard and Donald Walsh?

The undersea world and its marvelous life had been exposed by Barton and Beebe. But the ocean was far deeper than the level to which the two men had descended. One problem that prevented them from exploring deeper was the length of the steel cable that connected them to the surface. A Swiss scientist, Auguste Piccard, designed a craft called a bathyscaphe. Like a submarine, it could float free of any ship, but it was designed to withstand the crushing water pressure

Mapping the Ocean Floor

Unlike earlier mapmakers, who had to see the objects they were surveying for maps, oceanographers have been able to chart the mountains and valleys of the seabed with sonar. Sonar sends out an acoustical pulse, which bounces off an object and returns. By measuring the elapsed time between the pulse and its return, scientists can determine the depth of the ocean floor. Other sonar can be used to record impressions on the floor itself—peaks, ridges, and trenches.

of the deep ocean. In 1958, the United States Office of Naval Research purchased Piccard's bathyscaphe, which he called the *Trieste*. From then on, Piccard's son, Jacques, and navy engineers worked together to uncover the secrets of the deep.

In January 1960, Piccard and an American, Donald Walsh, prepared for a dive to the deepest known spot in the world's oceans—the Challenger Deep in the Marianas Trench in the Pacific Ocean—36,198 feet below sea level. On the day of the dive, the seas pitched and heaved, soaking the two men as they clambered aboard the *Trieste*. Minutes later, the sub descended into the depths. At 2,400 feet, the last rays of sunlight disappeared. At 18,000 feet, the small craft sprung a leak, but the enormous water pressure on the hull squeezed the metal shut. At 29,000 feet, Piccard dumped iron ballast from the sub, slowing the descent. Just past 35,000 feet, the men detected the return of a sound signal, indicating that the bottom was near. At 35,800 feet, *Trieste* settled gently on the seabed. At that depth, the pressure was a crushing 16,000 pounds per square inch. Walsh and Piccard peered through the windows for signs of life. There, on the muddy floor, Piccard spotted a flatfish eighteen inches long. Even here, life existed. After 20 minutes, the men set the *Trieste* in motion toward the surface. At 4:56 P.M., they broke the ocean surface, having gone just 398 feet short of the deepest spot on earth.

Who was Jacques Cousteau?

Jacques Cousteau was a Frenchman who revealed to the world the incredible and complex life beneath the ocean's surface. As a student at the French Naval Academy in the 1930s, Cousteau suffered an injury in an automobile accident that left his right arm paralyzed. A friend suggested he swim to rehabilitate his arm. He did, and wearing goggles, Cousteau saw "a jungle of fish. That was like an electric shock." Cousteau adapted a camera to take pictures underwater and he began thinking about a way for people to breathe underwater. At that time, divers breathed oxygen through a tube connected to a boat. It was cumbersome and dangerous. Cousteau developed the Aqua-Lung, an oxygen

Jacques Cousteau (left), with his son Phillipe, during the shooting of "The Singing Whale," an episode of the *The Undersea World of Jacques Cousteau.*

tank strapped to the back of the diver that allowed him or her to swim freely.

In 1951, Cousteau sailed in a ship, *Calypso*, to investigate the world's oceans. He improved the Aqua-Lung and built a camera capable of photographing life 600 feet deep. On his first voyage, to the Red Sea in 1952, he filmed and took photographs of amazing undersea life. He made a film, *The World of Silence*, out of his undersea clips, which won an Academy Award in 1955. He is best known for his television show, *The Undersea World of Jacques Cousteau*, which ran four times a year and lasted from 1966 to 1975. But Cousteau didn't remain happy to just film the ocean; he wanted to colonize it. Cousteau thought of the sea as a place to be colonized using craft similar to stations in space. In 1963, Cousteau and four other men spent a month at 33 feet beneath the Red Sea off the coast of Egypt in an underwater settlement that included air conditioning and Plexiglas windows that showed ocean life swimming by. His dreams of colonizing the ocean never materialized, but when Cousteau died in 1997, he was remembered as a passionate defender of the world's oceans. The Cousteau Society, founded by Cousteau in 1973, continues to fight for the protection of the environment and natural resources.

Who was Sylvia Earle?

Sylvia Earle was born in 1935 and raised on a farm in southern New Jersey, where she developed a passionate interest in nature. When she was ten, her family moved to Clearwater, Florida, a town on the coast of the Gulf of Mexico. She was fascinated by the ocean and its teeming life. Later at Florida State University, she learned to scuba dive and decided to study botany, the science of plant life. In 1964, she spent six weeks with a National Science Foundation expedition in the Indian Ocean. She also continued to catalog the marine plant life of the Gulf of Mexico, writing a detailed thesis for her Ph.D. that was widely read in the scientific community. In 1970, Earle became a national figure when she led an all-female research team to live 50 feet below the ocean surface in a structure called Tektite II, Mission 6. Earle used this fame to make films and write articles about marine life and the damage pollution caused to the world's oceans. In 1979, Earle wore a pressurized "Jim suit" and walked on the ocean floor 1,250 feet below the ocean surface off the Hawaiian islands. No other person has repeated the feat.

Who searched for *Titanic*?

On August 31, 1985, the research vessel *Knorr* patiently searched the bottom of the North Atlantic for the wreck of *Titanic*, a famous British luxury liner. More than 12,000 feet below the *Knorr*, a remote vessel called the *Argo* trailed along, sending images of the bottom to the *Knorr*. But after five weeks, the crew had seen little but an endless sheet of mud on the ocean floor. Aboard the *Knorr*, American Robert Ballard was co-commander of the search, and he realized with despair that the coming winter would shortly force him to return to port in failure.

An artist depicts the luxury liner *Titanic* as it takes its final plunge in the Atlantic Ocean in April 1912, a disaster that left more than 1,200 passengers and crew dead. The wreck of *Titanic* was found on the seafloor in 1985. The *Titanic* did not sink in one piece; it broke apart shortly before slipping beneath the surface.

Soon after midnight on September 1, Ballard went to bed, exhausted after weeks of fruitless searching.

How did Ballard find *Titanic*?

Just after 1 A.M., a crewman woke Ballard. *Argo's* cameras had spotted something. Ballard hurried to the video room, where television monitors showed the ghostly image of a huge, round metallic object. It was one of *Titanic's* boilers, the metallic drum that burned coal and gave the ship power. Ballard reasoned that it must have broken free when

Titanic

Titanic, a giant and beautiful ocean liner, struck an iceberg and sank in the chilly waters 400 miles south of Newfoundland in April 1912 on its maiden voyage. The ship, thought to be unsinkable, did not carry enough lifeboats for all passengers and crew. More than 1,200 of the 2,200 on board perished. The tragic scene of the ship sinking alone still grips the world's imagination decades after the tragedy.

Titanic sank and that the massive hull of the ship must be nearby. *Titanic* had been found. *Argo* was pulled north over a massive field of debris. Wine bottles, pots, dishes, and twisted pieces of jagged metal had been showered over a large area after *Titanic* broke in half shortly before sinking. A day later, *Argo* loomed over the bow section of the mighty ship, rising like a cliff out of the seabed. Speechless, Ballard and his crew stared at the giant, and still inspiring, ship, now covered in rust. Before Ballard left the site, he held a memorial service for those who had died in the disaster and placed a memorial plaque on the ship. Ballard's life changed forever after the *Titanic* discovery. Already a distinguished scientist and deep sea diver, he began a career of finding sunken ships, including the German battleship *Bismarck* and the American aircraft carrier *Yorktown*, both of which had been sunk during World War II.

egions? • Who were Robert Peary and Matthew
Henson? • How did Peary and Henson reach the North
Pole? • Who was the
first person to reach the South Pole? • When did Scott
reach the South Pole? • What happened to Scott? •
Who was Shackleton? How did Shackleton
try to cross Antarctica? • How did Shackleton save his
men? • Who was Louise
Arner Boyd? • Who was Annie Smith Peck? • Who
were George Mallory and Andrew Irvine? • How was
Mallory found? • Who was Sir Edmund Hillary?

INTO THE LANDS OF ICE AND SNOW

Why did explorers journey into the Arctic and Antarctic regions?

By the late 1800s, most of the earth had been mapped and explored. Explorers, eager to seek out new lands and adventures, looked to the frozen ice caps. But the lands of ice and frigid waters were also deadly. In 1848, a 129-man English exploration party journeyed into the Arctic on two steam-powered ships. They were never seen again.

The seasons change so swiftly in these extreme climates that explorers could find their ships quickly locked in ice several feet thick. And as the cold increased, the ice swelled, shifted, and could grind the ship into splintered pieces, leaving the crew marooned in a frozen wasteland.

Despite the dangers, explorers couldn't restrain their curiosity and their sense of adventure. The polar regions offered few material rewards or riches. Instead, each adventurer hoped to be the first man or woman to set foot on the North Pole and claim the glory for him- or herself and for his or her country.

Who were Robert Peary and Matthew Henson?

In spring 1909, the American explorer Robert Edwin Peary left the northern edge of western Canada with 24 men, 19 sleds, and 133 dogs. A veteran explorer of the polar region for 18 years, Peary was about to realize his dream— to become the first man to reach the North Pole. Following

Matthew Henson is shown dressed in the protective gear he needed to explore the icy polar regions. Henson accompanied all of Robert Peary's major explorations and led one of the parties on Peary's famous journey to the North Pole.

a well-organized plan, Peary planned to dash 413 miles across the ice. But, as Peary observed, the Arctic ice is not "a gigantic skating pond with a level floor over which the dogs drag us merrily." The ocean currents fractured the ice, creating huge cracks of black seawater called "leads" that could delay a party for weeks. The ocean also slammed huge blocks of ice together, piling them into a ridge that could be 50 feet high. An advance party hacked its way through these obstacles to make a path for the following parties.

Matthew Henson, an African American explorer who had participated in all of Peary's major expeditions, led one of the parties. Henson ran away from his home in Washington, D.C., when he was 12. He became a cabin boy and spent the next six years traveling all over the world on ships. After he returned to Washington, Henson worked as a clerk in a clothing store. One day, a man walked in to buy supplies for an expedition to Nicaragua. The man mentioned that he needed supplies and a servant. The store owner told him about Henson, who had experience traveling around the world. The man, Robert Peary, was impressed and took Henson with him. He proved so essential to the expedition that Peary later remarked, "I couldn't get along without him." To prepare for the trip to the North Pole, Henson studied the Eskimo language and culture.

How did Peary and Henson reach the North Pole?

At first, the group journeyed about ten miles a day. At night, they slept in snug igloos built from blocks of snow. But after traveling 45 miles, Peary was halted by a jagged crack of black sea that snaked for miles through the ice. Peary called it the "Big Lead" and waited impatiently for it to freeze over or for the ice to close back together. Days passed, his Eskimo helpers talked about leaving, and Peary fretted that his expedition was doomed. After seven long days, the lead froze over, and the party hurried north. As he had planned, Peary began sending back the weaker dogs and men to the ship, allowing the main party to continue quickly. By April 1, only 133 miles of ice separated Peary from his goal. Five days later, after traveling more than 25 miles a day, Peary, Henson, and four Eskimo companions reached the Pole. In triumph, Peary took out an American flag sewn by his wife, nailed it to a staff, and planted it at the top of a snow pile. To confirm the discovery, Peary continued north another ten miles, until he noticed that he was no longer traveling north but south. He had passed the Pole. With the trail made and igloos already constructed, the return trip to their ship at Cape Sheridan on Ellesmere Island took only 16 days. By mid-July, the expedition was safe and sailing south, and Peary telegraphed the world of his success.

Robert Peary, bundled up for warmth, poses with some of the sled dogs after his successful expedition to the North Pole.

Who was Roald Amundsen?

Roald Amundsen, a Norwegian explorer, was startled when he learned of Peary's feat. Since he was a young boy, Amundsen had dreamed of being the first man to the North Pole. He had even been preparing a voyage when the news of Peary's triumph reached him. To salvage the funds and energy already invested in the expedition, Amundsen abruptly changed his plans. Instead of seeking the North Pole, he resolved to reach the South Pole in Antarctica, where no man or woman had yet set foot.

In 1911, Amundsen directed his ship, the *Fram*, into the Ross Sea, just off the coast of Antarctica. For the first part of the year, Amundsen and his men unloaded supplies and built camps. Just 400 miles to the west, a group of

English explorers led by Robert Falcon Scott also prepared to reach the Pole. The journey to the South Pole had become a race.

Who was the first person to reach the South Pole?

On October 19, 1911, Amundsen led four sleds, each pulled by 13 dogs, into the icy wilderness of Antarctica. Amundsen had spent many years in the frigid regions of the earth and had learned to wear the clothing of Eskimos. He also followed a simple but harsh belief: "Don't treat your men like dogs or your dogs like men." To conserve food, he shot the weaker dogs as the journey lengthened and used the meat to feed both his men and the animals. The party spent an agonizing number of days pulling the sleds over the Queen Maud mountain range. But with the mountains behind them, the worst of the trip was over. Nearly two months after leaving the base camp, the expedition had reached the southernmost spot reached by another explorer, and only 97 miles remained. "I had the same feeling that I can remember as a little boy on the night before Christmas Eve—an intense expectation of what was going to happen," wrote Amundsen later. At 3 P.M., December 14, the jubilant party recorded that they were at 90 degrees South Latitude—the South Pole. For four days, they took measurements. Before leaving, they raised a Norwegian flag and left a note for the English party, which they were sure would be arriving soon. Slightly more than a month later, Amundsen and his men were back safely aboard the *Fram*. They had won the race.

When did Scott reach the South Pole?

Robert Scott was determined to reach the South Pole before Amundsen and claim it both for his glory and that of his native England. But Scott made serious miscalculations. While Amundsen used dogs to pull his sleds, Scott opted for ponies. After leaving his base on October 24, the expedition struggled through a landscape of stone and ice. The Queen Maud mountain range broke sleds and left both the men and animals exhausted. Within five weeks, the ponies were dead or shot for meat. Then a howling blizzard stopped the expedition, leaving the men huddling in their tents and burning precious fuel. Finally, in January, Scott and four other men harnessed themselves to a sled and dragged it to the final destination. There they met bitter disappointment. Amundsen's tent and the Norwegian flag greeted them. "The Norwegians have forestalled us and are the first at the Pole. It is a terrible disappointment, and I am very sorry for my loyal companions," wrote Scott in his journal.

What happened to Scott?

Their morale sunk, the five-man group began the long trek back. But hunger, injuries, and exhaustion slowed their progress as they dragged the sled across the frozen terrain. By February, the continent was again sliding into winter, sending temperatures plummeting. The expedition slowed to a crawl. On February 17, one of the men fell into a coma and died. In the following weeks, the men began to starve. In March, they were caught in a howling blizzard. One of Scott's companions, L. E. G. Oates, suffered such severe frostbite in his feet that he could scarcely walk. Realizing that he was slowing the expedition, Oates turned to the other men in the tent and told them he was going to go outside. "I may be some time," he added and then disappeared into the swirling snow, never to be seen alive again. "We knew it was the act of a brave man and an English gentleman," wrote Scott in his journal. The three survivors continued to struggle north, but in vain. A blizzard locked them in their tent. Unable to move and realizing that death was imminent, Scott wrote letters to his wife, to his mother, to friends, and a "Message to the Public." His final entry in his journal is dated March 29. Eight months later, a rescue party discovered the three bodies still inside the tent. The party also recovered Scott's journal, and his name became a symbol around the world of courage in the face of death.

Who was Ernest Shackleton?

Along with Scott and Amundsen, Ernest Shackleton was one of the world's greatest polar explorers. From 1901 to 1904, Shackleton accompanied Scott into the Antarctic. In 1907, he returned, this time in command of his own expedition and determined to be the first man to the South Pole. Like Scott, Shackleton preferred ponies to dogs. He took ten with him, but two perished before he landed on the continent and another seven died from the cold or from eating volcanic grit in the snow. Still, Shackleton and three companions pressed on. A crevasse suddenly opened underneath the expedition and the last pony disappeared into the gaping crack. Shackleton led the men for another month, up to a plateau 11,200 feet above sea level, where a blizzard forced them into their tent for 60 hours. "We simply lie here shivering," wrote Shackleton. If one of their feet was frozen, they placed it on the skin of their companion to warm it up again. The cold was too much. Just 97 miles from the Pole, Shackleton turned back. He returned to his native England a hero, but also, as a newspaper described him, a "splendid failure."

How did Shackleton try to cross Antarctica?

After Amundsen reached the South Pole, Shackleton decided to lead an expedition across Antarctica, something that no one had done before. Shackleton, 27 men, and 69 dogs boarded a ship called the *Endurance* and sailed in December 1914. By the end of January, the *Endurance* had sailed through miles of pack ice surrounding the continent and could go no farther. Winter came, sunlight dwindled, and the ice thickened, grinding against the ship's wooden hull. For ten months, the men waited for a break in the ice, but none came. In October, the ice crushed the ship's hull, shattering it into splinters while the men watched. But under Shackleton's leadership, the expedition did not despair. They salvaged the ship's lifeboats and some of the supplies. When the weather warmed again, they rowed through the deadly currents and ice floes, finally arriving

Would You Answer This Ad?

In 1914, Shackleton placed an advertisement in the *Times* of London, requesting volunteers for his journey to Antarctica. It read:

Men Wanted for Hazardous Journey. Small wages, bitter cold, long months of complete darkness, constant danger, safe return doubtful. Honour and recognition in case of success.

—Ernest Shackleton

The doomed ship *Endurance* heels over under the pressure of Antarctic ice, which would eventually grind her to pieces. The crew, led by Ernest Shackleton, salvaged the lifeboats and some of the supplies and eventually reached Antarctica. They were rescued 18 months later.

on the continent in April 1916. Joyful that they had survived, the men also contemplated that they had no way off the continent and not enough supplies to complete their expedition across it.

How did Shackleton save his men?

On April 24, Shackleton and five other men set out to do the impossible. Leaving the rest of the party behind, they set out in a 22-foot boat to reach the island of South Georgia, off Argentina and more than 800 miles across the frigid Antarctic Ocean. The tiny craft climbed giant waves and then plunged into troughs again and again, soaking the crew in freezing water. "The sub-Antarctic Ocean lived up to its evil reputation," Shackleton later wrote. One night, a 60-foot tidal wave roared into the boat, practically sinking it. "We baled with the energy of men fighting for life," wrote Shackleton. Somehow, the tiny craft survived. For 14 days, the men fought the sea and, after food and water ran out, their thirst and hunger. Finally, they sighted the island. Two days later, Shackleton steered the tiny craft up onto the beach of South Georgia. But their ordeal wasn't over. After drinking fresh water and feasting on tiny chicks nesting nearby, Shackleton and the men began an incredible trek through icy mountainous terrain to reach an isolated whaling post on the other side of the island. It took them 36 hours. The whalers were astounded when the bedraggled men stumbled into town. Shackleton had been missing for two years and all had assumed he was dead. After briefly enjoying the whalers' admiration, Shackleton arranged to pick up his remaining men—first, those left on the other side of South Georgia, then those on Antarctica. At the end of August, Shackleton sighted the party and asked if any had died. None, came the reply. Shackleton was indeed one of the most successful failures in exploration history. He wrote to his wife, "Not a life lost and we have been through Hell. . . . Give my love and kisses to the children. Your tired 'Mickey.'"

Who was Richard Byrd?

Born into a Virginia family in 1888, Richard Byrd from the start lived a life of exploration and adventure. At the age of 12, Byrd traveled alone to the Philippines to visit his godfather. In letters he wrote back to the local newspaper, he described public hangings and gunfire aimed at him by rebels. Byrd later joined the navy and trained to become an aviator. The new technology excited Byrd, and he realized that a plane could carry a pilot to the North Pole and back in under a day. Byrd failed in several attempts to make the journey while he was still with the navy. At age 38, Byrd raised funds for his own trip.

In April 1926, Byrd traveled from New York to Spitsbergen, Norway, in a ship with 52 men and an airplane. He hoped to be the first person to fly to the North Pole. But on his first attempt, the skis under his plane collapsed. On the second try, however, Byrd and his pilot, Floyd Bennett, climbed steadily into the arctic sky. Despite an oil leak, the pair flew on toward the Pole. After more than eight hours, Byrd and Bennett circled the Pole and returned. The American press described Byrd as a hero, and he received a ticker-tape parade in New York City. The foreign press, however, wondered how Byrd could have reached the Pole and returned in the time that he did. Doubts about whether Byrd truly reached the Pole persist to this day.

Byrd still became a national hero. Congress awarded him and Bennett the Congressional Medal of Honor. Within a year, Byrd announced another adventure—to fly over the South Pole. In autumn 1928, four ships carrying Byrd, three planes, 42 men, and 650 tons of supplies steamed toward Antarctica. The expedition was watched closely in the press. The *New York Times* even prepared Byrd's obituary. The men established camp and waited out the Antarctic winter. On Thanksgiving Day 1929, Byrd and pilot Bernt Balchen took off. "What we faced far surpassed the demands of a simple flight of 800 miles to the Pole," Byrd later wrote. "We would fly over a barren, rolling surface, then climb a mountain rampart and continue across a 10,000-foot plateau. . . . Before us, beyond the great mountains, lay uncertainty."

But the plane flew safely on, and Byrd calculated that they had reached the South Pole. The news was relayed to the world and Byrd, once again, was proclaimed a hero.

In 1933, Byrd returned to Antarctica, this time to map portions of the continent and claim land for the United States. In a controversial strategy, Byrd spent five months alone in a tiny hut, enduring temperatures between −58° F and −76° F. "I see my whole life pass in review. I realize how I have failed to see that the simple, homely, unpretentious things of life are the most important," he wrote in his diary. Byrd, suffering from carbon monoxide poisoning and frostbite, had to be rescued.

Byrd returned to Antarctica several more times over the next two decades, usually at the head of U.S. naval and scientific explorations. He mapped much of the Antarctic coast, and he remains an aviation hero and one of the great explorers of the continent.

Who was Louise Arner Boyd?

Louise Boyd, an American heiress, inherited a vast fortune in 1920 when she was 33. Uncertain what to do with her life or her wealth, Boyd boarded a Norwegian tour boat on a summer cruise to the Arctic. The rugged, austere landscape fascinated her. She soon returned in a chartered ship, this time hunting polar bears and photographing the scenery. In 1928, an Italian aviator named Umberto Nobile attempted to fly over the Arctic in a blimp. The craft crashed and Roald Amundsen took off in a plane to rescue the aviator. Nobile was found and saved, but Amundsen disappeared. Boyd joined the international search to find the explorer by loaning her ship to the rescue effort and spending four months looking for him. Amundsen, however, was never seen again. For her rescue attempts in the Arctic, Boyd was awarded France's Cross of the Legion of Honor and Norway's Chevalier Cross of the Order of Saint Olav.

Her experience searching for Amundsen also inspired her to become an explorer in her own right. In 1931, she began an intense study of the fjords in Greenland. Her work impressed American scientists and was supported by the American Geographical Society. In 1955, Boyd hired a plane and became the first woman to fly over the North Pole. In 1960, her contributions to exploration were recognized when she was elected to the American Geographical Society, the first woman to receive that honor.

Who was Annie Smith Peck?

Born in Providence, Rhode Island, during the 1850s, Annie Smith Peck acquired a competitive attitude that drove her to accomplish great things in her lifetime. In 1885, Peck traveled from Germany to Athens, Greece, where she planned to study classical literature. On the journey, she glimpsed the Matterhorn, a 14,692-foot mountain in the Swiss Alps. The rocky, snow-crusted peak gripped her imagination. She longed to climb it.

After returning to the United States, she began practice climbs on small mountains. In 1888, she climbed 14,162-

foot Mount Shasta in California. She returned to Europe and climbed the Matterhorn in 1895, becoming famous. Peck gave up her teaching career and concentrated on mountain climbing full-time. Two years after conquering the Matterhorn, Peck climbed Mount Orizaba, a volcano in Mexico that rose more than 18,406 feet. It was the highest point in the Western Hemisphere reached by a woman. But Peck wasn't satisfied with being the first *woman* to reach the top of a mountain. She wanted to be the first *person* to

Annie Smith Peck poses for this photograph with some of the gear she used to scale mountains.

reach a summit. She traveled to South America, where many peaks had not yet been explored. In 1908, 58-year-old Peck and two Swiss guides struggled through snowdrifts to reach the 22,205-foot summit of Mount Huascarán in Peru. When they reached the top of the mountain, Peck thought joyfully that she would be the first person to climb the peak. But one of her guides dashed past her and ran to the summit. Peck could only claim to be the first woman to the top. Despite the disappointment, Peck continued climbing mountains, scaling her last peak at the age of 82. In 1927, the Lima Geographical Society honored her by naming the north peak of Huascarán Cumbre Aña Peck.

Who were George Mallory and Andrew Irvine?

George Leigh Mallory was a skilled English mountain climber who decided to attempt the "Third Pole"—Mount Everest in the Himalaya Mountains, at 29,028 feet, the highest mountain in the world. When asked repeatedly why he wanted to climb Mount Everest, Mallory answered, "Because it's there." In June 1924, Mallory, 38, and a companion, 22-year-old Andrew Irvine, using oxygen bottles to breathe in the thin air at that high elevation, approached the summit. Noel Odell, a geologist, stayed in a lower camp and watched them climb higher up the mountain. Shortly after noon on June 8, Odell glimpsed them—just specks now—climbing when a bank of clouds swirled in. A sudden storm covered the peak in snow, and Odell waited vainly for their return. Mallory and Irvine were never heard from again.

How was Mallory found?

For decades, people wondered whether the doomed pair had reached the top of Mount Everest before dying. In *The Fight for Everest 1924*, published shortly after the disaster, Odell wrote, "I think myself there is a strong probability that Mallory and Irvine succeeded."

In 1933, Irvine's ice axe was found at 27,750 feet. In 1975, a Chinese climber named Wang Hongbao reported having seen a body about 750 feet below where the ice axe was found. When he touched the clothing on the body, said Hongbao, it disintegrated—indicating that it was very old.

Relying on Hongbao's story, in 1999 a team of American, English, and German climbers and scientists searched for Mallory's body at an elevation of about 27,000 feet. In May, an American climber named Conrad Anker spotted a patch of white that seemed brighter than the surrounding snow. When Anker looked closer, he discovered a body that had been dead for a long time and preserved in the thin, frigid air. At first, the expedition believed they had found Irvine. They searched the body for a camera that Irvine was known to be carrying. If Mallory and Irvine had reached the summit of Everest, they would have certainly taken pictures of the event. But on the collar of the corpse's shirt was stitched "G. L. Mallory." The body was Mallory's, not Irvine's. The expedition also noted that Mallory must have suffered a serious fall that broke his legs, ribs, and elbow. After burying Mallory, the expedition descended the mountain. Although Mallory had been found, the mystery of whether Mallory and Irvine were indeed the first to reach the summit remains unanswered.

Who was Sir Edmund Hillary?

Sir Edmund Hillary was a rugged New Zealander who in 1953 stepped onto the top of the world—the 29,028-foot summit of Mount Everest. Many climbers had attempted to climb Mount Everest. But the high altitude was treacherous. The weather could change quickly. A clear sky could suddenly fill with clouds and 100-mile-per-hour winds. The air was so thin that climbers needed to carry oxygen tanks, or else the lack of oxygen to their brains would cause climbers to become disoriented and possibly black out. Muscles, which also needed oxygen, exhausted quickly. Two men, George Leigh Mallory and Andrew Irvine, had approached the summit in 1924, but they were never seen again. In 1953, a British-organized expedition of ten men tried again. Hillary, an enormous man who exuded confidence, was among them.

Who was Tenzing Norgay?

In March 1953, the members of the British expedition to Mount Everest, along with 350 porters, ascended to a Buddhist monastery called Thyangboche in Nepal. At

13,500 feet above sea level, the monastery became the expedition's first base camp. From there, Hillary and the other men took hikes into the surrounding mountains to become acclimatized to the high altitude before the attempt would be made on Mount Everest. Hillary quickly formed a partnership with Tenzing Norgay, a member of the Sherpa tribe who lived in the Himalayas and who was a veteran of five trips to Mount Everest. During their first climb together, Hillary slipped into a crevasse. Tenzing quickly maneuvered the rope that connected them and pulled Hillary out of the crevasse. "Without Tenzing, I would have been finished today," Hillary said back at camp. The two men became fast friends.

Edmund Hillary and Tenzing Norgay became the first two men to ascend the summit of Mount Everest. Their climbing experiences led to a deep friendship.

How did Tenzing and Hillary reach the summit of Mount Everest?

The expedition established camps at higher and higher altitudes—19,400 feet, 20,200 feet, 23,000 feet, and 24,000

Between 1953 and May 1996, 630 climbers reached the peak of Mount Everest. Another 144 died trying.

feet. On May 26, two members of the team climbed to 28,700 feet and pushed on almost to the summit. But the sun set, and the exhausted, frozen pair stumbled back to camp. The next day, Hillary and Tenzing made an attempt. They climbed to 27,900 feet and pitched a tent to spend the night and recoup their strength for a final push the next morning. Though the wind died down that night, Hillary's boots were frozen solid in the morning. After a breakfast of sardines, biscuits, and lemon juice, the two men set off up a steep slope covered in snow. They hacked steps into the crust, finally making their way to a boulder 40 feet high that blocked their way to the crest. The rock was too smooth to climb and blocked on the left. But on the right, Hillary and Tenzing climbed a narrow crack that Hillary compared to a narrow chimney. At the top, Hillary, with Tenzing close behind, climbed a snowy ridge and stood at last at the top of Mount Everest. The two men hugged each other with joy and beheld the staggering view that stretched before them. They remained at the summit about 15 minutes before picking their way back down the mountain's face to the camp, where their companions waited in excitement.

Who was Reinhold Messner?

Reinhold Messner didn't just climb mountains, he conquered them the hard way—alone, without oxygen, or at record speed. Born and raised in northern Italy, Messner began scaling the peaks of the eastern Alps as a teenager. After climbing more than 500 mountains in Europe, the 30-year-old Messner led an expedition to the Andes Mountains

The Sherpas

About 20,000 Sherpas live in Nepal. Most of them make their home in villages in Khumbu, a region in the shadow of Mount Everest. Because they spend most their lives between 9,000 and 11,000 feet and are accustomed to the thin atmosphere, the Sherpas were hired to carry supplies and equipment for the first expeditions up Everest. They soon developed a reputation for strength, endurance, intelligence, and good humor. Today, Sherpas regularly accompany groups up the mountain and are relied upon as guides.

in South America in 1974. There, he climbed the 22,834-foot Aconcagua Mountain. He completed the last 10,000 feet of the climb alone. In 1978, Messner attempted a feat that shocked the climbing community. He proposed climbing Mount Everest without oxygen. No one can climb at such altitudes and survive without oxygen bottles, said critics. But Messner was undeterred. He and a companion, Peter Habeler, arrived in a base camp below the mighty face of Everest in March 1978. By May, they camped at nearly 24,000 feet. The air was so thin that the two men gasped for breath. Because their muscles desperately needed oxygen, simple movements demanded great energy and concentration. On the morning that Messner and Habeler prepared to reach the summit, it took them two hours to get dressed. Every breath of air was precious, and the pair stopped speaking and communicated with hand signals. Still, they climbed higher, pausing for a rest every few steps. Messner later wrote that he felt an exhaustion and numbness he had never experienced before. Sometime after noon on May 8, Habeler and Messner struggled over the crest and reached the top of Mount Everest. Their daring climb astounded the world. The next year, Messner climbed K2, the world's second-tallest mountain, without oxygen. By 1982, Messner had completed an even greater feat—he had climbed the world's tallest 14 peaks, all over 26,250 feet, without oxygen. He returned to his native Italy as the greatest climber in history.

Who were the first explorers of flight? Who were the first people to fly in a balloon? Who was Otto Lilienthal? How did the Wright brothers make their first flight? How did the Wright brothers make their first flight? How did Charles Lindbergh fly solo across the Atlantic Ocean? Who was Amy Johnson? Who was Amelia Earhart? Who was the first person to break the sound barrier? What was the Space Race? Who was first person into space? What was "the Right Stuff"? Who was John Glenn? Who was the first woman in space? Who was Neil Armstrong? Who was the first man on the moon? Who was the first American woman

SOARING HIGH ABOVE

Who were the first explorers of flight?

For thousands of years, men and women have looked at birds soaring overhead and dreamed that they might one day join them. In the Middle Ages, a monk named Oliver crafted a glider with two wings. With the contraption strapped to his back, he leaped from a tower, sailed "125 paces," and fell heavily to the earth, breaking both legs. Marco Polo told stories of Chinese who rode in giant kites. Leonardo da Vinci, the great Italian thinker of the sixteenth century, left sketchbooks full of flying machines, including a rough plan for a parachute. In the 1670s, a French locksmith named Besnier tried to fly by pumping two poles with flaps over his shoulders. He, too, fell to the earth. In 1670, a Jesuit priest named Francisco de Lana Terzi concluded from experiments that air has weight. Therefore, he theorized, it could be possible to construct a craft with a huge globe that was lighter than air—a balloon.

Who were the first people to fly in a balloon?

In 1782, two French brothers named Joseph and Étienne Montgolfier were sitting in front of a fire when they noticed ashes billowing upward, carried by the heated air. They came to a startling conclusion. If the heated air could be captured in a large enough bag, it might be strong enough to carry a person. On June 4, 1783, the brothers lit a pile of straw and wool beneath a ball made of linen lined

Benjamin Franklin
watched the first
manned free flight
in a balloon from his
terrace in Paris, France,
in 1783. He later made
this engraving to com-
memorate the event.

with paper. The ball caught the hot air and sailed upward,
to about 6,000 feet. Delighted by their achievement, the
Montgolfiers built another, larger balloon with a basket
underneath. In front of 130,000 spectators, including the
king and queen of France, the brothers put a sheep, a roost-
er, and a duck in the basket, used hot coals to heat air into
the balloon, and let it loose. The balloon traveled two miles
in eight minutes and carried the animals to earth safely.
After this success, the brothers set out to construct a balloon
that would carry humans. Using blue cotton cloth, they
fashioned a craft 70 feet high, 46 feet in diameter, and
weighing 1,600 pounds. On November 21, 1783, two
Frenchmen, Pilatre de Rozier and the Marquis d'Arlandes,

boarded the basket beneath the balloon and were cut free from the earth. The balloon climbed slowly, and at 300 feet the two men doffed their hats to the awed crowd watching them. Then the wind pulled them over Paris and they reached an altitude of 1,650 feet. They watched in amazement as the people moved beneath them as tiny as insects. After 25 minutes, the trip ended, and they landed softly on the ground. For the first time in history, two men had successfully flown.

Who was Otto Lilienthal?

Flying balloons became enormously popular in Europe and the United States. But several Europeans turned their attention to building a heavier-than-air aircraft. In 1889, a German named Otto Lilienthal published a book on designing flying machines based on the wings of birds. To test his theories, Lilienthal constructed an artificial hill. From the top, he could leap into the direction of any oncoming wind. His flights were thrilling but brief. Lilienthal's gliders were fatally flawed. He tried to steer his craft by shifting his weight, which tended to compound his errors. If the glider jerked upward, Lilienthal swung back, causing the glider to flip over. But Lilienthal was persistent, and he made more than 2,000 flights in gliders of his own construction. He was killed after a crash in 1896, having failed to produce a stable glider. But his ideas would influence two bicycle makers in Ohio named Orville and Wilbur Wright.

How did the Wright brothers make their first flight?

The Wright brothers grew up in Dayton, Ohio, where they operated a bicycle shop. Neither of the Wright brothers finished high school, but they were curious and disciplined, and they became fascinated by flight. In the late 1890s, they collected information on flight and set out to solve the problems that still stymied inventors around the world. The Wright brothers built their first glider in 1899. From the weather service, they learned that Kitty Hawk, North Carolina, enjoyed almost constant winds. In 1901, the Wright brothers painstakingly brought their glider to Kitty Hawk and began a number of test flights. Through

At Kitty Hawk, North Carolina, Wilbur Wright watches as his brother, Orville, makes the first flight of a controlled, powered aircraft. The first flight lasted 12 seconds and traveled 120 feet.

trial and error, they created a steering mechanism, but the wings still didn't respond as they had calculated. They returned to their bicycle shop in Ohio and built a wind tunnel to conduct precise tests on each wing section. From the tests, the Wrights learned that most published figures on wind and flight—the figures they had used when building their first craft—were incorrect. They built a new glider based on their tests, brought it to Kitty Hawk, and flew it successfully.

By 1903, they only needed an engine for the glider to become an airplane. Characteristically, the brothers took elements of existing engines and redesigned them into a lighter and more efficient engine. On December 17, 1903, Orville lay down on the lower wing to take the aircraft's controls. With the engines powering two propellers, the craft slid down a track on the beach and was airborne. It flew 12 seconds and landed softly in the sand 120 feet away. Now Wilbur took a turn, flying the airplane almost 200 feet. By the end of the day, the plane had flown 59 seconds and 852 feet. The first controlled flight of an airplane had occurred.

Bessie Coleman, turned down by every flight school in the United States, learned to fly in France. Coleman's dreams of founding a school of aviation for African Americans ended with her death in a flight accident in 1926.

Who was Bessie Coleman?

In 1921, Bessie Coleman, born to a poor African American family in Texas, moved to Chicago, where she became interested in flying. After being turned down by almost every flight instructor in the country, she went to France and earned her pilot's license. Because she was African American, Coleman was not allowed to fly commercial aircraft in the United States. Instead, she became a barnstormer, flying a World War I fighter plane in a series of dazzling stunts and maneuvers that spread her fame throughout the country. Coleman encouraged African American interest in aviation by speaking at African American churches and schools. She was raising money to found a school of aviation for African American students when she was thrown from her airplane and killed in 1926.

How did Charles Lindbergh fly solo across the Atlantic Ocean?

After World War I, daredevil pilots flew planes to their limits, setting records and then breaking them. A man named Raymond Orteig offered $25,000 to the first person to fly solo from Paris to New York. The trip was very dangerous. The pilot's engine could fail, a sudden weather change could slam his or her plane into the ocean, or he or she could fall asleep at the controls and crash. Two Frenchmen had attempted the flight in 1927 and disappeared over the Atlantic. Despite the odds, Charles Lindbergh, a shy, soft-spoken pilot from the Midwest, decided to try. Lindbergh secured financing from some St. Louis businessmen, who insisted that he name his plane after their city. He agreed, calling the plane *Spirit of St. Louis*.

Lindbergh's plane was more of a flying gas tank than anything else. He had modified a passenger plane by cramming all the extra space with fuel tanks. When Lindbergh took off from Roosevelt Field, New York, on May 20, 1927, he steered by peeking through a periscope. For the next 33 hours, Lindbergh flew his tiny plane over the lonely Atlantic. When he began to doze, he pinched himself or opened the side window and scooped icy air into the cabin. After flying more than 22 hours, he scanned the ocean and spotted some fishing boats before continuing on, exhausted. Finally, he glimpsed the brilliant green coast of Ireland. He had made it! As he flew south over England, Lindbergh's plane was spotted and news spread across the continent. When he landed in Paris, Lindbergh was greeted by roaring crowds. By flying 3,614 miles, he had broken the solo distance record. A worldwide hero, Lindbergh used his influence to help develop aviation in the United States.

Who was Amy Johnson?

On May 5, 1930, Amy Johnson took off from England on one of the boldest journeys in aviation history. Though she had earned her pilot's license only a year before, Johnson planned to fly alone from England to Australia. Her route would take her across Europe, over the Middle East, India, the East Indies, and then the open ocean before she reached Australia. Johnson's plan stunned other pilots. Much of the route was over jungle or mountain ranges with little hope of rescue if she crashed. Her plane could fly no higher than 10,000 feet, so she would have to maneuver through mountain ranges with peaks much higher. During her journey, she ran into a sandstorm over Syria, blinding her and forcing her to make an emergency landing. In some places where she stopped, men wouldn't allow her near the engine, even though she was a skilled mechanic. They had never seen a woman repair her own aircraft. In Burma, she patched a hole in her wing with shirt fabric. Nearing complete exhaustion, Johnson flew the final 500 miles over the sea and landed in Darwin, Australia, on May 24, 1930. Johnson accomplished other daring and dangerous flights during the 1930s, earning her the nickname "Air Queen." Tragically, she was killed in an accident in 1941.

Who was Amelia Earhart?

When American Amelia Earhart earned her pilot's license in 1922, she was one of 22 female pilots in the world. Determined to prove that women could fly as well as men, she planned to fly solo across the Atlantic Ocean. On May 20, 1932, she took off in a bright red Lockheed

Amelia Earhart, one of the best known female aviators of the early days of flight, poses between the propellers of her Lockheed Electra plane. Earhart vanished during a flight over the Pacific Ocean.

Vega from Newfoundland. Only two men, Charles Lindbergh and Bert Hinkler, had made the solo flight across the Atlantic successfully. Earhart carried an elephant foot bracelet for good luck, a flask of soup, and a silk scarf. She also carried a powder compact to touch up before speaking to reporters. If she felt herself dozing off, she put smelling salts under her nose. Soon after she took off, her altimeter broke, leaving her with no way to measure her altitude. She flew into a storm, which buffeted her tiny plane. She flew higher to escape the storm, but ice collected on the wings, which threatened to make her lose control. To remove the ice, she plunged into a quick dive and straightened up just above the reach of the waves. Her airplane stayed aloft, and 14 hours and 56 minutes after taking off, she landed safely in a farmer's field in Ireland. Earhart's Atlantic flight made her famous. In 1935, she flew alone from Hawaii to California. In 1937, she planned to fly around the world with a copilot. But during the 2,500-mile trip over the Pacific Ocean, contact with Earhart's plane was lost. She, her copilot, and the airplane were never seen again. Most likely, Earhart was lost in the fog and crashed after running out of fuel.

Who was the first person to break the sound barrier?

World War II fighter planes reached top speeds of 600 miles per hour. After the war, jet engines dramatically increased airplane speed. Some people wondered if pilots could maneuver or even survive flying so fast. Others theorized that any plane attempting to fly faster

The Ninety-Nines

In 1929, the greatest female aviators from around the world competed in the eight-day Women's Air Derby. On November 2, 1929, the aviators formed an association of women fliers called the Ninety-Nines, named after the number of charter members. Amelia Earhart was the association's first president. The Ninety-Nines published *The 99-er*, a magazine that featured the achievements of female aviators and discussed the latest advances in aeronautics.

than the speed of sound, or Mach 1, would run into a wall of air and shatter. On October 14, 1947, a B-29 bomber roared aloft above the deserts of southern California. Inside the plane's hatch was a 31-foot, bright orange jet airplane that looked like a bullet. The Bell X-1 was designed to withstand the pressures of flying beyond the speed of sound. American pilot Chuck Yeager climbed down into the tiny cockpit and at 20,000 feet, the plane was released. Yeager activated the first rocket, which slammed him back into his seat. One by one, additional boosters ignited, pushing the aircraft's speed to .7 Mach, .8 Mach, and finally to the edge of the sound barrier. Below, observers heard a giant explosion that echoed through the desert. Yeager had broken the sound barrier, producing the first sonic boom in history. Yeager's flight paved the way for supersonic jets and the space program. Pilots would never again wonder what existed on the other side of the sound barrier.

What was the Space Race?

After World War II ended in 1945, the United States and the Union of Soviet Socialist Republics (U.S.S.R.) competed to become the most powerful nation in the world. The rivalry extended to many areas—industrial power, military strength, and achievement in the arts and sciences. Space became a vast testing ground, a place where one society could prove its superiority over the other. In 1957, the Soviets launched *Sputnik I*, the first man-made satellite to

Faster than the Speed of Sound

The speed of sound is known as Mach 1. However, sound can travel through the atmosphere at varying speeds at different places and times, depending on the air pressure and air temperature. Experiments and calculations in 1986 determined that at freezing temperatures, in dry air, sound travels about 741.1 miles an hour. At around 60 degrees Fahrenheit, sound travels faster—about 760 miles an hour. When Chuck Yeager flew his Bell X-1 and broke the sound barrier, the speed of sound in his area was 662 miles per hour. His craft eventually reached Mach 1.06, or about 700 miles an hour.

orbit the Earth. The Soviets were triumphant and the United States was stunned. Since then, both nations have devoted enormous resources and manpower to achieving milestones in space. The race was on.

Who was first person into space?

On April 12, 1961, a young Russian cosmonaut named Yury Gagarin boarded a capsule atop a giant rocket at Baikonur, the Soviet space center in south-central Kazakhstan. The rocket blasted off, carrying Gagarin where no human had ever traveled and returned safely—space. In his tiny capsule, called the *Swallow*, Gagarin soared 200 miles above Earth. For a few minutes, he marveled at the beauty of the sphere beneath him. But *Swallow* soon reentered Earth's atmosphere. Gagarin landed safely in a potato field outside the Russian city of Saratov. In a 108-minute flight Gagarin had orbited Earth once and returned. It was a stupendous feat. The 28-year-old Gagarin was heralded as Hero, First Class, of the Soviet Union and recognized around the world. Streets all over the Soviet Union were renamed in his honor. Gagarin planned to return to space but he was killed in a jet crash in 1968.

Who had the "right stuff"?

In 1959, NASA (the National Aeronautics and Space Administration) began an extensive process to select the United States' first astronauts. The agency looked for jet pilots with more than 1,500 hours' flight experience. The astronauts had to be younger than 40 years old, in excellent shape, and shorter than 5'11"—to fit into a small space capsule. NASA also wanted college graduates or people with engineering degrees. More than 500 applicants met these requirements. In April 1959, after several months of intense physical and psychological tests, NASA picked seven men to be the first American astronauts: Navy Lieutenant M. Scott Carpenter; Air Force captains L. Gordon Cooper, Jr., Virgil I. "Gus" Grissom, and Donald K. "Deke" Slayton; Marine Lieutenant Colonel John H. Glenn, Jr.; and Navy lieutenant commanders Walter M. Schirra, Jr., and Alan B. Shepard, Jr.

Who was John Glenn?

When Gagarin orbited Earth, NASA was pressing ahead with its own plans to put men into space. Two American astronauts—Alan Shepard and Virgil Grissom—flew rockets into the atmosphere and returned safely. But none orbited Earth. For that mission, NASA selected John Glenn. On February 20, 1962, at Cape Canaveral, Florida, Glenn boarded the *Friendship 7*, a tiny capsule at the end of a towering Atlas rocket. In a blast of searing light, the rocket's engines propelled Glenn and the *Friendship 7* into the atmosphere. In a flight that lasted five hours, Glenn circled the world three times. When he passed over the city of Perth, Australia, at night, the people of the city turned on their lights to greet him. Although the steering system malfunctioned, Glenn guided the craft back into the atmosphere and landed safely in the Atlantic Ocean, north of Puerto Rico. Glenn was a national hero. In 1974, he became a senator from Ohio and ran for president ten years later. In 1998, the 77-year-old Glenn returned to space for the first time in more than 30 years when he flew with the space shuttle as part of a series of experiments on space travel and the elderly.

Who was the first woman in space?

In 1961, the Soviet Union accepted 24-year-old Valentina Tereshkova for cosmonaut training. Tereshkova, who had made more than 126 parachute jumps, trained for two years. Though Tereshkova was not as well trained as other female Soviet pilots, she was accepted because the Soviet leader, Nikita Khruschev, wanted an ordinary worker. Tereshkova was not well educated, but she studied hard and was able to pass grueling tests of physical endurance. On June 16, 1963, Tereshkova, the first woman to enter space, was carried into Earth's orbit aboard the *Vostok 6*. "I see the horizon," she said over the radio. "A light blue, a blue band. This is the earth. How beautiful it is. Everything is going well." Over three days, Tereshkova circled the globe 48 times, totaling 1,255,000 miles. She returned to Earth safely and was awarded Hero of the Soviet Union and received the Order of Lenin.

Astronaut Neil Armstrong snapped this picture of fellow astronaut Edwin Aldrin Jr. and the U.S. flag during the first landing of men on the moon on July 20, 1969. The Lunar Module *Eagle*, which carried the astronauts to the surface, is visible on the left. Armstrong and Aldrin would spend 21 hours and 37 minutes on the moon taking photographs, collecting samples, and setting up scientific equipment.

Who was Neil Armstrong?

Neil Armstrong began a love affair with airplanes and flying as a young child in Ohio. He earned his pilot's license before he earned a high school diploma. Later, he flew 78 combat missions as a fighter pilot during the Korean War. After the war, Armstrong completed a degree in aeronautical engineering and joined the National Advisory Committee for Aeronautics, which became the National Aeronautics and Space Administration (NASA). As a test pilot, Armstrong flew the rocket-powered X-15, a plane that reached speeds of 4,000 mph and heights 40 miles above the earth's surface. In 1962, Armstrong was selected to become an astronaut. In 1966, he flew his first mission in space in *Gemini 8*.

Who was the first man on the moon?

For his next mission, Armstrong was selected to lead Apollo 11, NASA's first attempt to land on the moon. For years, the space agency had sent craft deep into space to orbit the moon. This time, they intended to accomplish a feat that human beings had dreamed of for thousands of years—to touch the moon.

On July 16, 1969, a mighty Saturn V rocket thundered off the launch pad at Cape Kennedy, Florida, carrying Armstrong, Michael Collins, and Edwin "Buzz" Aldrin into space. Three days later, the command spacecraft, called *Columbia,* and the landing craft, the *Eagle,* entered the moon's orbit. After another three days, Armstrong and Aldrin steered the tiny *Eagle* onto the gray moon surface, while Collins remained aboard *Columbia.* Millions watched on television as Armstrong opened the *Eagle's* outer door and climbed down the ladder, stiff in his bulky spacesuit.

The Dangers of Space

The exploration of space has claimed the lives of 15 men and women. On January 27, 1967, three American astronauts, Virgil Grissom, Edward White II, and Roger Chaffee, were strapped into a capsule atop a rocket for a takeoff simulation. At 6:31 P.M., a frantic voice cried out that a fire had started in the capsule. Within seconds, the fire spread, fueled by the highly flammable pure oxygen pumped into the capsule. The heat was so intense that fire crews took five minutes to break open the capsule. But by then, the three astronauts were dead.

Another major American space disaster occurred in 1986 on the space shuttle *Challenger.* Rockets thundering, the space shuttle soared nine miles into the atmosphere. But 73 seconds into the flight, a devastating explosion shattered the space-

craft and sent it hurtling to the earth. An investigation later found that synthetic rubber seals between the sections of the fuel tank had failed. Burning fuel had leaked through the gap, causing the explosion. Seven astronauts were killed, including the first civilian, Christa McAuliffe.

The Soviet Union has also suffered from accidents. In 1967, Vladimir Komarov blasted into space. But the ship tumbled, causing the parachutes to tangle. When Komarov streaked toward Earth, the parachutes failed to open, and the ship slammed to the ground, killing him. In another disaster, three Soviet cosmonauts completed 23 days of experiments in space in 1971. When they landed on Earth, a faulty hatch exploded open. The sudden decompression killed all three instantly.

His boot ground into the soft powder, leaving a print that was shown around the world. "That's one small step for man," he said, "one giant leap for mankind." For the next two and a half hours, Armstrong and Aldrin trotted over the moon's surface, planted an American flag, and placed scientific instruments to measure the moon's environment. They returned to the *Columbia*, reentered Earth's atmosphere, and splashed down safely on July 24, 1969.

Who was the first American woman in space?

In 1977, a 26-year-old woman named Sally Ride read an announcement that NASA sought young scientists to work on the space shuttle. Ride had graduated from Stanford University in 1972 with a degree in physics and English and was working toward her Ph.D. Until then, NASA relied on military pilots to staff their space program, but now they needed specialists to work on board the new space shuttle. More than 8,000 people applied to the program, about 1,000 of them women. Ride was selected to be part of a group of 35 new astronauts and soon underwent training to receive her pilot's license. On June 18, 1983, Ride became the first American woman in space. As a mission specialist aboard the *Challenger*, Ride tested a mechanical arm in space that was designed to release and retrieve satellites. She also was flight engineer, assisting the pilot during takeoff and reentry. "The thing that I'll remember most about the flight is that it was fun," she said. "In fact, I'm sure it was the most fun I'll ever have in my life."

Who are Dick Rutan and Jeana Yeager?

Dick Rutan and Jeana Yeager met at an airshow in Chino, California, in the late 1970s. Both of them were experienced pilots. Rutan had started taking flying lessons when he was 15 and had earned his pilot's license a year later. He then served as a navigator and fighter pilot in the Air Force during the Vietnam War. After leaving the Air Force, he became a test pilot for his brother, Burt, an airplane designer. Yeager earned her pilot's license in 1978 and also became a test pilot for the Rutan Company. In 1981, Yeager and Burt and Dick Rutan sat at lunch and discussed building a plane that could fly around the world

Sally Ride works in the weightless atmosphere of the space shuttle. Ride, the first American woman in space, was selected by NASA from an applicant pool of more than 8,000.

without stopping or refueling. For the next five years, Burt drew up designs for the aircraft while Yeager and Dick raised money to build it. They called the airplane *Voyager*.

How did Rutan and Yeager fly the *Voyager* nonstop around the world?

Burt designed the *Voyager* in a large H shape, with the main wing in the rear. The wing, at 111 feet, was longer than the wingspan of a 727 passenger airliner. Burt used light materials made from epoxy and engines that drove the craft 80 miles per hour. While one pilot guided the controls, the other rested in a narrow cabin three feet wide. In July 1986, Dick and Jeana flew the plane up and down the California coast for four and a half days, covering 11,000 miles. On December 14, 1986, Dick and Jeana took off from Edwards Air Force Base in California to fulfill their dream of flying around the world. While one pilot slept for two or three hours at a time and ate precooked meals, the other steered the *Voyager* toward the Pacific. They ran into a typhoon near the Philippines that buffeted the plane and propelled it to 147 miles per hour. They hit more storms over India, shaking the plane so violently that Yeager was badly bruised. Another near disaster occurred on the coast of Africa, when Dick momentarily lost control of the aircraft. Yeager guided the plane in the dark over Central America. On December 23, 1986, Dick landed the plane at Edwards Air Force Base, one day ahead of schedule. They had done it. In nine days, they had circled the world without stopping or refueling. Yeager and Dick were awarded the Presidential Citizen's Medal by President Ronald Reagan and the *Voyager* was hung in the Smithsonian's National Air and Space Museum in Washington, D.C.

Who were the first to fly nonstop around the world in a balloon?

Incredibly, even as late as the 1990s, no one had claimed the prize of being the first to fly around the world in a balloon. The "Great Balloon Race," as it was called, attracted aviators and wealthy adventurers. Several crews attempted to break the record in the 1990s. One landed in the Pacific Ocean near Hawaii after running low on fuel. Another was drenched in rainstorms and was forced down near Japan. No one was seriously injured during these trips, but others were not so fortunate. In 1995, two balloonists were killed when they were shot down over Belarus in Asia. Belarus officials thought the two men were on a spy mission.

In March 1999, a Swiss named Bertrand Piccard and his partner, Brian Jones, from Great Britain, took off from Switzerland. Their balloon did not resemble traditional hot-air balloons. Instead, the two men rode in a pressurized capsule called the *Breitling Orbiter 3*. The capsule protected them as the balloon carried them to 36,000 feet. Inside the balloon were sections containing helium gas and another pocket that could be filled with hot air. By heating the air and dropping ballast, Piccard and Jones could control their altitude and search for wind currents that would carry them in the correct direction. The wind carried the balloon at an average of 130 miles an hour across southern Europe, North Africa, Southeast Asia, the Pacific Ocean, Central America, and finally across the Atlantic and Africa. The voyage was perilous. At night, the water in the capsule froze, and Piccard knocked away ice that clung to the balloon and threatened to drag them down. On March 20, the balloon passed Mauritania far to the south of Switzerland, but on the same line of longitude —where they began the journey—and the two men celebrated. With a sense of drama, they tried to land their craft triumphantly near the pyramids of Egypt. But rough winds forced them to land in the sands of the Sahara desert near an isolated village. Piccard and Jones were exhausted. The team had remained aloft for 19 days, 21 hours, and 55 minutes and covered a distance of 29,055 miles. The distance broke an endurance record and won them a $1-million prize from the Anheuser-Busch company.

GLOSSARY

A
adobe a heavy clay used to make bricks in the American Southwest
arable fit for planting crops
astrolabe an instrument used to measure the angle of heavenly bodies, e.g., the Moon, Sun, and stars

B
balloon an aircraft made up of a large ball of silk or plastic. It flies when the ball is filled with lighter-than-air gasses.
bathysphere a craft used for deep sea exploration
botany the science of plant life
Buddhism a religion that originated in India and Eastern Asia. Buddhism taught followers to seek enlightenment through denial of earthly passions.

C
capsule a small sealed cabin designed for flight above the atmosphere
caravel a ship used in the 1400s, with two large masts and triangular sails. Columbus sailed in a caravel.
circumnavigate to sail completely around the world or an island
compass an navigational instrument that indicates magnetic north
conquistador a Spanish or Portuguese who conquered Mexico and South America during the 1400s, 1500s, and 1600s
coral a species of sea animal that secretes a hard skeleton, usually in shallow, warm ocean waters. Coral can build into reefs that extend hundreds of miles.
cosmonaut Russian astronaut
crevasse a crack or break in glacial ice
curragh a boat made from animal skins

G
glider an aircraft without a motor that flies on air currents

L
lead a gap in the Arctic ice caused by ocean currents
longitude a measurement, made in degrees, running east and west, starting at Greenwich, England

M
Mach 1 the speed of sound

magnetic north the direction a compass points to. Magnetic north does not align precisely with the North Pole.

meteorologists scientists who study weather and weather patterns

monarch sole ruler of a country, such as a king, a queen, or an emperor

mutiny a rebellion against officers and authority, usually on a ship at sea

N

nao a ship used in the 1500s and 1600s with three large masts and square sails. Magellan sailed in a nao.

Northwest Passage a channel through North America to the Pacific Ocean. Explorers searched for it through the 1600s and 1700s, but it did not exist.

R

rapids a place in a river where water descends swiftly, usually over bare rocks

rigging the ropes and cables that hold up a ship's sails

S

scurvy disease caused by the lack of Vitamin C and leading to bleeding and blackened gums. It was especially common among sailors on long journeys during the 1600s and 1700s.

smallpox a deadly disease caused by a virus and often leading to severe scarring of the skin

sound barrier the drag on a jet as it approaches the speed of sound. Some thought that no plane could fly past the sound barrier, or Mach 1.

T

trading post a frontier store where Indians, settlers, and trappers could trade for goods

trailblazer a person who goes off all paths and creates a new trail

W

wingspan length of a wing from tip to tip

SELECTED BIBLIOGRAPHY

Allen, Oliver E. *The Seafarers: The Pacific Navigators*. Alexandria, VA: Time-Life Books, 1980.

Boorstin, Daniel J. *The Discoverers: The History of Man's Search to Know His World and Himself*. New York: Random House, 1983.

Boyne, Walter J. *The Smithsonian Book of Flight*. Washington, D.C.: Smithsonian Books, 1987.

Davis, Lee. *Man-Made Catastrophes: From the Burning of Rome to the Lockerbie Crash*. New York: Facts on File, 1993.

Debenham, Frank. *Discovery and Exploration: An Atlas—History*. Garden City: Doubleday, 1960.

Diamond, Jared. *Guns, Germs, and Steel*. New York: W.W. Norton, 1997.

East, W. Gordon. *The Geography Behind History*. New York: W.W. Norton, 1965.

Goodman, Edward J. *The Explorers of South America*. New York: Macmillan, 1972.

Hanbury-Tenison, Robin. *The Oxford Book of Exploration*. New York: Oxford University Press, 1993.

Heacox, Kim. *Shackleton: The Antarctic Challenge*. Washington, D.C.: National Geographic Society, 1999.

Hibbert, Christopher. *Africa Explored: Europeans in the Dark Continent 1769–1889*. New York: W.W. Norton, 1982.

Hochschild, Adam. *King Leopold's Ghost*. New York: Houghton Mifflin, 1998.

Hornblower, Simon, and Anthony Spawforth. *The Oxford Companion to Classical Civilization*. Oxford: Oxford University Press, 1998.

Humble, Richard. *The Seafarers: The Explorers*. Alexandria, VA: Time-Life Books, 1978.

Konstam, Angus. *Historical Atlas of Exploration: 1492–1600*. New York: Checkmark Books, 2000.

Krakauer, Jon. *Into Thin Air: A Personal Account of the Mt. Everest Disaster*. New York: Doubleday, 1997.

Lacey, Peter, ed. *Reader's Digest Great Adventures That Changed Our World*. Pleasantville, NY: Reader's Digest, Inc., 1978.

Lewis, Richard S. *Appointment to the Moon: The Inside Story of America's Space Venture*. New York: Viking, 1968.

Middleton, Dorothy. *Victorian Lady Travellers*. New York: Dutton, 1965.

Olds, Elizabeth Fagg. *Women of the Four Winds*. Boston: Houghton Mifflin, 1985.

Palmer, Robert Roswell, and Joel Colton. *A History of the Modern World*. New York: McGraw-Hill, 1992.

Phelps, J. Alfred. *They Had a Dream: The Story of African-American Astronauts*. Novato, CA: Presidio Press, 1994.

Prescott, Jerome. *100 Explorers Who Shaped World History*. San Mateo, CA: Bluewood Books, 1996.

Rasky, Frank. *The North Pole or Bust*. New York: McGraw-Hill Ryerson Limited, 1977.

Riverain, Jean. *Concise Encyclopedia of Explorations*. Chicago: Follett, 1969.

Rabinowitz, Harold. *Conquer the Sky: Great Moments in Aviation*. New York: Metro Books, 1996.

Scott, Phil. *The Shoulders of Giants: A History of Human Flight to 1919*. New York: Addison-Wesley, 1995.

Sobel, Dava. *Longitude: The True Story of the Lone Genius Who Solved the Greatest Scientific Problem of His Time*. New York: Penguin Books USA, 1996.

Spufford, Francis. *I May Be Some Time: Ice and the English Imagination*. New York: Picador USA, 1997.

Stefoff, Rebecca. *Women of the World: Women Travelers and Explorers*. New York: Oxford University Press, 1992.

Wilcox, Desmond. *Ten Who Dared*. Boston: Little, Brown, 1977.

Wright, Louis B. *Gold, Glory and the Gospel*. New York: Atheneum, 1970.

Wright, Louis B. and Elaine Fowler, ed. *The Moving Frontier: North America Seen Through the Eyes of Its Pioneer Discoverers*. New York: Delacorte, 1972.

———. *West and by North: North America Seen Through the Eyes of Its Seafaring Discoverers*. New York: Delacorte Press, 1971.

THE NEW YORK PUBLIC LIBRARY'S RECOMMENDED READING LIST

Anderson, Madelyn Klein. *Robert E. Peary and the Fight for the North Pole.* New York: Watts, 1992.

Armstrong, Jennifer. *Shipwreck at the Bottom of the World.* New York: Crown, 1998.

Blumberg, Rhoda. *Incredible Journey of Lewis and Clark.* New York: Lothrop, Lee & Shepard, 1987.

Explorers: From Ancient Times to the Space Age. New York: Macmillan Reference, 1999.

Faber, Harold. *Discoverers of America.* New York: Scribner, 1992.

Hull, Mary. *Travels of Marco Polo.* San Diego, CA: Lucent, 1995.

Lilley, Stephen R. *Hernando Cortes.* San Diego, CA: Lucent, 1996.

Matthews, Rupert. *Explorer.* New York: Knopf, 1991.

Neal, Valerie. *Spaceflight: A Smithsonian Guide.* New York: Macmillan USA, 1995.

Noonan, Jon. *Captain Cook.* New York: Crestwood House, 1993.

Sensevère-Dreher, Diane. *Explorers Who Got Lost.* New York: Tor, 1992.

Stefoff, Rebecca. *Ferdinand Magellan and the Discovery of the World Ocean.* New York: Chelsea, 1990.

Twist, Clint. *Magellan and da Gama.* Austin, TX: Raintree Steck-Vaughn, 1994.

West, Delno. C. *Christopher Columbus.* New York: Atheneum, 1991.

White, Alana. *Sacagawea: Westward with Lewis and Clark.* Springfield, NJ: Enslow, 1997.

Worth, Richard. *Stanley and Livingstone and the Exploration of Africa in World History.* Berkeley Heights, NJ: Enslow, 2000.

INDEX

PHOTOGRAPHY CREDITS

pp. 8–9, U.S. Bureau of Public Roads; p. 10, Picture Collection, The Branch Libraries, New York Public Library; p.14, Universitätsbibliothek, Heidelberg, Germany; p. 17, Picture Collection, The Branch Libraries, New York Public Library; p. 30, Picture Collection, The Branch Libraries, New York Public Library; p. 33, Picture Collection, The Branch Libraries, New York Public Library; p. 37, The Granger Collection, New York; pp. 42–43, Prints and Photographs Division, Library of Congress; p. 47, Picture Collection, The Branch Libraries, New York Public Library; p. 53, Picture Collection, The Branch Libraries, New York Public Library; pp. 54–55, Rare Books and Maps Division, Library of Congress; pp. 58–59, Rare Books and Maps Division, Library of Congress; p. 60, Picture Collection, The Branch Libraries, New York Public Library; p. 63, From the Collections of the St. Louis Mercantile Library at the University of Missouri-St. Louis; pp. 66–67, Geography and Map Division, Library of Congress; p. 68, Royal Geographical Society, London; p. 69, Courtesy of the Bancroft Library, University of California, Berkeley; p. 75, Manuscripts, Archives and Rare Books Division of the Schomburg Center for Research in Black Culture, New York Public Library, Astor, Lenox and Tilden Foundations; p. 78, Picture Collection, The Branch Libraries, New York Public Library; p. 81, Prints and Photographs Division, Library of Congress; pp. 84–85, Geography and Map Division, Library of Congress; p. 86, Picture Collection, The Branch Libraries, New York Public Library; p. 88, Oriental Division, New York Public Library, Astor, Lenox and Tilden Foundations; pp. 92–93, Geography and Map Division, Library of Congress; p. 96, Bettman/Corbis; pp. 98–99, Geography and Map Division, Library of Congress; p. 103, Bettman/Corbis; p. 105, Picture Collection, The Branch Libraries, New York Public Library; p. 108, Bettman/Corbis; p. 110, Bettman/Corbis; p. 114, Royal Geographical Society, London; p. 118, Prints and Photographs Division, Library of Congress; p. 121, Hulton Deutsch Collection/Corbis; p. 126, Picture Collection, The Branch Libraries, New York Public Library; p. 128, Prints and Photographs Division, Library of Congress; p. 129, Underwood & Underwood/ Corbis; p. 131, Picture Collection, The Branch Libraries, New York Public Library; p. 136, National Aeronautics and Space Administration; p. 139, National Aeronautics and Space Administration